BRED IN THE HIGHLANDS

Ben Coutts' previous books include:

Bothy to Big Ben
Auld Acquaintance
A Scotsman's War

All are available from Mercat Press

BRED IN THE HIGHLANDS

Ponies, Cattle and Folk

BEN COUTTS

MERCAT
PRESS

First published in 1997 by Mercat Press
James Thin, 53 South Bridge, Edinburgh EH1 1YS

ISBN 1873644 68X

Typeset in Bembo at Mercat Press
Printed and bound in Great Britain by
Redwood Books, Trowbridge, Wiltshire

Contents

Illustrations

The late Duke of Atholl presenting the prizes to the winners of the Working Highland Pony class at the Scottish Farmer *Highland Pony Show, 1994. Blair Castle can be seen in the background (Niall Robertson)*

Dedication

The photo opposite is of Iain, the late Duke of Atholl, presenting the prizes at the first working Highland Pony Class, sponsored by the *Scottish Farmer* and held in front of Blair Castle, which can be seen in the background. I was doing the commentary on this occasion and His Grace sat in my caravan for most of the day. I told him I was about to write this book, and asked him, as his forebears had bred both Highland cattle and ponies, and one had written the preface to John MacDonald's book on Highland ponies, would he be kind enough to do the same for me? His reply was immediate. 'Ben, sadly modern farm practices don't allow the Estate to keep Highland cattle, since the upkeep of the Estate depends on the farming enterprise as one of its profit-making units. But as for our Highland Pony Stud, with our popular trekking centre going from strength to strength, I want to establish it as a really first-class stud. So of course I'll write a preface.' Sadly, the 'Reaper' took Iain last year, and I lost a good friend, and a benefactor too, as he allowed me a small share in a racehorse, something I had always wanted but couldn't afford. Because of the foregoing I wish to dedicate these ramblings to the memory of a soft-spoken, shy Highland gentleman, a first-class Highland Laird, the late 5th Duke of Atholl.

Acknowledgements

This book has been written, not as a handbook for the Highland Pony and Cattle Societies, but as a record of the experiences and the thoughts the author has had about his connection with these breeds, their societies and the folk involved with them during the last half century. I apologise to the cognoscenti of both breeds who will feel I have left out certain breeders' names who should have been included, but it would be impossible to mention everyone.

My thanks to all suppliers of information or photos for the book go without saying. With regard to those who supplied pictures, credit has been given in the caption accompanying each photo. With regard to those who gave information, two or three who provided a lot of information are not mentioned in the book, notably Bruce Cheape and Alison Bartholemew, who virtually made the Mull chapter for me, and I would like to thank them here. To the delightful team on Rhum who wanted me to go to stay on the island to see the ponies and cattle there, can I say how I would have loved to take up their invitation, but by that stage I had already spent more than I'll receive in royalties in travelling round and gathering information for the book. As to postage and telephone calls, the less said the better.

To my great supporter and harshest critic, my dear wife Sal, as always, my thanks. As a terrific Highland pony enthusiast she will no doubt take me to task over some of my comments on the breed and its breeders.

My thanks to Isabel Johnstone who once again has done a super typing job for me.

Thanks also to the respective secretaries of the Highland Cattle and Pony Societies for their help.

Tom and Seán of Mercat Press can, if cajoled, give me the odd 'lunch on the house': but much more importantly, they knew where to insert the photos I produced and were able to edit my thoughts, the punctuation of which all too often needs attention. We have become friends, and I've enjoyed working with them: I am only sorry that this will be my last book. I thank them for their backing and co-operation.

Finally, thanks to the Chileans. As far as I am aware they know nothing of Highland ponies and cattle, but their wine has an affinity with the author's pen and ink and puts 'notions in his heid' which he puts into print.

To all the above my thanks, and of course to all those I have written up in the book. I know I won't make money out of the book, but as country life has changed and is changing so rapidly, I hope to preserve a bit of history for the years to come. If I have done so successfully, thanks are due to all who have contributed to the book in any way.

1
Ponies, Cattle and Folk

All my life the Highlands have to me been like honey to a bee. I just love them, for all their vagaries of climate. I love the people who live there and with whom I've had the privilege to work, whose motto all too often is, 'When the Lord made time he made plenty of it'. A motto that many down in the Home Counties, who dash from pillar to post, could adopt to their advantage—but one which can be very frustrating if you are trying to get a job completed before the next lot of rain soaks you, which it invariably does in summer time in the Highlands.

In modern times tourism is the industry on which successive Governments have spent money, but it is an activity that depends on the weather, and at very best has only four good months in which to operate. But the three Fs, Farming, Fishing and Forestry, have been the mainstay of the Highland economy since the Second World War, and the farming side goes back hundreds of years. The Highland cattle of Scotland were the mainstay of the Highland economy. The famous Crieff and Falkirk Trysts had thousands of cattle taken there every year by the 'tacksmen' of each district. These would need to have been very honest men (but I'll bet there was the odd twister), as they took the cattle from the crofters to sell them at a Tryst and had to return with the 'readies', real cash in hand, to the owner.

Old 'Corrie', alias John Cameron of Corriechoilie, in Lochaber, must be the most famous of those who took cattle to the Trysts. Back in the nineteenth century he took two thousand Highland cattle and twenty thousand sheep to a Falkirk Tryst! The mind boggles as to how he organised that number of animals to be herded, some from Caithness and Sutherland and many from the Islands, down the non-existent roads of one hundred and fifty years ago. Just imagine what we in the Army called the commissariat, i.e. the feeding for all those beasts and the men who were droving them! He must have been fantastically fit, as he personally supervised all his flocks and herds to the Trysts. For these trips he rode a famous piebald (black and white) mare which many believe was one of the foundation stock of the Gaick Highland Pony Stud. So even all those one hundred years and more ago the lives of Highland Folk, Cattle and Ponies were intertwined.

How tremendously fit those men who walked the cattle to the Trysts must have been, and on only sparse rations. I've herded cattle but short distances compared with those super chaps of whom all too little has been recorded. The 'Chief', Corrie, has been written up, and like all big men had a 'fair conceit o' himsel'. The story is told, and I know it to be true, that he was working with his cattle and sheep on one of his many hill farms when he accidentally fell into the adjacent burn, which because of melting snow and a south-west wind and rain, a bad combination in the West Highlands, had become a raging torrent. Corrie, who like all hill men of that period (and later) hardly ever bathed, never mind learned to swim, was being washed away. Just in time he managed to grab the overhanging branch of a tree and pulled himself onto the bank, where his faithful shepherd, a devout church-goer, was standing. The shepherd exclaimed, 'You'll need to get down on your knees and thank God for your deliverance.' Corrie's reply was typical of many successful people, like so many today, whose only thought is of themselves and financial gain—'Well, I didn't do too badly mysel'!'

And talking of hill men not being swimmers I remember as a laddie being sent in an ancient bull-nosed Morris Cowley (so-called because the radiator had a bullish appearance) to fetch a head keeper from the pub in St Fillans, after the hotel manager had phoned the keeper's wife to say that he had been rescued from the river Earn. I remember, as if it was yesterday, that madam was NOT amused: however as she didn't drive I was despatched to get the fu', very 'drookit' boss, because that's what he was to me at the time. During the two mile journey back to his abode he kept repeating to me, 'If I wasn't a swimmer I'd have been drowned.'

I got him home, pushed him in the door, and judging by the row that met him felt sorry for the wee man—because he was wee, and she was huge, just like a ship in full sail! I went back next day to see the said river and it was two feet deep!

One more story about hill men and their aversion to water. On an estate I managed there was a loch over which the stalker had to row to reach the stalking ground and bring back the stags or hinds. The stalker, a super old character, had taken on a 'Holy Joe' bible thumper as his ghillie. When they were coming back one January day, after overloading the boat with hinds, the loch suddenly erupted as Highland lochs can, as I well know. I have experienced it all too often myself when the wind suddenly comes whistling down the glens surrounding those lochs. On this occasion the boat was nearly gunwhaled under because of the weight of hinds. The stalker, terrified, said to the ghillie, 'You're always taking about your great saviour— get down on your knees and pray, pray for us to be saved now!' Whereupon the ghillie got down on his knees in the boat and began: 'Oh, Lord, who sent his son to calm the Sea of Galilee...' At which point the stalker interrupted him: 'This is no job for a laddie,' he said, 'Get the old man to come!'

Perhaps this is why I'm penning these reminiscences of the three Hs. People like that old stalker, the keeper 'on the spree' at New Year and old Corrie and their like made the Highlands, and they are people who will not be easily replaced. Those now wanting to do their jobs expect, because of TV and other modern media, to get many more material rewards.

But back to the Trysts, which of course were the forerunners of the modern auction marts. These sprang up in easily accessible centres to obviate the need to

The great Corrichoilie, leading sheep and cattle farmer of the Highlands in the nineteenth century (Iain M. Thomson)

Two pictures showing how much traffic conditions have changed in the Highlands. The top picture (A.C. Cowper) was taken in Perthshire in 1956, when the sight of a car was a rare event! The bottom picture (Ena MacNeill) shows a traffic-jam in modern-day Uist.

drove cattle and sheep hundreds of miles. This of course later became the norm thanks to modern transport: firstly the railway system and then road transport. The latter now uses huge lorries completely unsuited to many of our country roads—but such, they say, is progress.

Yet how quickly things can change. Whereas there were local marts dotted all over the British Isles, they are now being centralised. In my own area of central Perthshire, Crieff, so namely a seasonal mart in the days of the huge cattle droves, has now been closed down. Killin, which had one of the best autumn sales of cattle, many with fat-stock winter show potential, and Aberfeldy with its famous 'Spring' sale, have gone to the wall. (I remember asking the late Lovat Fraser, one of Scotland's greatest auctioneers, why the famous Aberfeldy sale, held in February when spring in that area was still three months distant, was called 'Spring' and he replied, 'Just because the spring and grass were so far away and the farmers had to sell stock to leave enough feed for their cows, which in those days were the only capital they had.')

So here we are now with fewer outlets for our stock in the Highlands than earlier in my lifetime, but there is a tremendous demand from overseas which deserves a chapter on its own. The sad thing is that the demise of the Trysts and local marts has taken away one of the main meeting places for those of us who look after the only thing we humans (who think we are so clever) can't make any more of, i.e. land. It was at markets and local shows that farmers met and discussed their business—which bull they should use on their Highland females (as in those days arable farmers wanted faster maturing stock—now they only want continental stock), or which stallion might suit their mares to get a pony with a better free-going action etc. Most importantly of all, the local mart was in its day the centre of all things to do with the land.

So times have changed with my subjects, Highland Cattle, Ponies and Folk. The Folk now depend on TV and radio for their advice and crack. The cattle depend on their pedigree potential, sadly most are now for overseas, but of that more later. The ponies also depend heavily on overseas demand, though despite this the Society have never countenanced a breed sale. I tried to get one going at the Highland Show, but it never took off.

The small marts going to the wall have altered many of our so-called market towns. Take the one which is nearest me, i.e. Crieff. When I came back from the war to manage farms in Strathearn, Tuesday was market day and the whole town was given over to the farming community. In the morning we had the livestock mart with sheep, cattle, yes, and pigs too. Then up we went to St James Square where we were met by representatives of the feed and fertiliser firms, although fifty years ago less of both these commodities was bought. At this time the feed was nearly all home-grown hay, straw, oats and turnips, all with a lot of labour and sweat, and with but little mechanical aid; and as for fertiliser, Nitrogen, which is now used in fantastic amounts, was little used and we depended on good old dung. This reminds me of the story about a farmer's daughter who had been sent off to a 'posh' private school from a fairly rough farm. This was because the hard-working farmer, who had married above his station, had made some cash during the war; and 'madam' had decreed that daughter should be educated away from the coarse locals. Daughter came back at a time when the cattle reeds were being emptied of their dung in the spring, and as usual in any farm household, the talk was of the seasonal work. Her mother kept talking about the 'dung', much to the daughter's annoyance, who finally burst out: 'Mother, you musn't use that coarse word, you ought to call it manure'. Back came mother's reply: 'You ought to have heard what your Dad called it before I married him!'

Then on those market days we farmers, or in my case farm managers, took our samples of oats, barley or wheat to show to the 'reps'. Meantime the ladies would do their shopping, and some would be bartering eggs and butter for the food they couldn't produce themselves. Nearly everyone in the Strath farms would have a house cow—I would be one of the last to milk a cow when I gave up mine nine years ago. At that time the shops in Crieff contained things one needed to maintain life: there were grocers, bakers, fishmongers, tailors, greengrocers, butchers, iron-mongers (most important to farmers in those days of manual labour) and tobacconists, as we all smoked then. Nowadays the town has antique shops, boutiques, florists, shops that sell what father called 'gee-gaws', things one doesn't need, endless tea shops and restaurants, sports shops etc. etc., and of course two supermarkets. I have nothing against any of those shops, but what I'm trying to say is that because of our completely different outlook today as to what we regard as essentials in our life the subjects of this book, the cattle, the ponies and the folk have changed dramatically. This has happened so quickly that as one of the last of my generation, and someone who can scribble a bit, I thought it essential that something of their past history as known to me should be recorded.

Highland ponies, called garrons by many, were an essential part of a Highland farm or croft and before mechanisation were used for all cultivations plus carting. They also conveyed the family to the local market town, and of course to the Kirk, as everyone went to church in the old days, changed days indeed. But now that we have tractors and four-wheeled-drive vehicles (the status symbol of the townees who have taken over many of the cottages that were once the habitat of farm workers), four-wheeled motor bikes, fore-loaders etc. the Highland pony has become an ani-mal mainly used for enjoyment, riding or driving.

Highland cattle, once the mainstay of the Highland economy, or it would be fairer to say Highland existence, for that's all the Highland folk could hope for two hundred years ago, were superseded by other breeds. Lowland farmers who bought the cattle found they could make more money by using quicker maturing breeds, firstly the Beef Shorthorn (known as the great improver) then the Aberdeen-Angus, still world famous for the texture and quality of its meat. This is something which Highland beef also has, but it takes a year longer to mature, and that takes a lot of extra money. Then farmers in the good finishing areas, usually down the east coast where the better land and drier climates are found, Aberdeenshire, Angus, Fife, the Lothians etc., and in England—Yorkshire, Lincolnshire etc.—those farmers wanted bigger cattle which would weigh more when killed. Because of this they turned to the Continental breeds: Charolais, Simmental, Limousin, Belgian Blues etc. The last is not one of my favourites, because to my way of thinking cattle should be able to thrive in their own country, and those cattle could not survive in the Highlands of Scotland, as their conformation is wrong. I'm told most have to have a caesarian operation to give birth—not an easy procedure if not totally impossible on a Scottish hill farm!

My wife complains bitterly when I say farmers who are making a lot of money out of a system with which I don't agree are being greedy. What I can't condone is farmers who opt for quantity, usually tasteless, rather than quality. For me, although I am 6 ft 3 ins (in my stocking holes), big is not beautiful. However, sadly, Highland cattle have drifted out of the mainstream of supplying maintenance to the Highland community and beef to the urban population, and more is the pity.

As for the folk, well one only has to look at the thousands of cottages which are occupied by those who have a good pension and have fled from the big cities with all their strains, their endless queues of traffic and their smell of vehicle fumes, the pushing and shoving in tubes and supermarkets, the high cost of living, especially of housing and oh! just everthing the true countryman abhors. Or they are used as holiday homes, though I always continue to think of them as a farmworker's or shepherd's cottage. But one can't turn the clock back, and one has to face the fact that we all want a high standard of living today, and I include myself. Although I stayed blissfully in a bothy (that was mentioned in the Domesday Book and had few improvements made to it until after the last war!) I now couldn't do without my central heating, double-glazing and a glass or two each night of something 'that gladdens the heart of man'.

Because we all want a higher standard of living—and compared with the late twenties and early thirties there is nothing like the poverty now that there was then—the vast majority in the Highlands are miles better off. To achieve this the hill farmers had to dispense with labour, as the workers were needing more pay, perquisites and holidays than of yore, which the farm couldn't stand if the farmer and his family were to get the standard of living *they* wanted. Hence the empty cottages, and in some cases, and there may be more to come, the empty hill farm houses.

So for many reasons the three subjects of this book are not playing the part they did two hundred years ago in the Highlands. In different ways, however, they are still playing a part in the Highland economy. Let's have a look at them individually as they have progressed over those years.

2
My Involvement with Highland Ponies

My interest in the Highland pony breed goes back a long way. In 1930 at the age of fourteen I 'plunked' school in Glasgow to visit the Highland Show and earn the princely sum of 2/6d (12½p) for looking after a Highland pony mare from the Derculich Stud. In those days one slept in the straw beside one's pony. At that particular show the Scots Greys were the main attraction. The groom in charge of the Derculich ponies had gone off to the bar, as then, even more than today, the Highland Show was the grooms' only holiday when they met their pals, swapped yarns and gossip and got gently, but never fighting, fu'!

The horse beside our straw-bedded area was the Derculich grey stallion, whose name escapes me, but I do remember his temperament was 'dodgy'. I was wakened by a Glasgow voice shouting, 'Stand still ye b——!' I shot out of my makeshift bedding (two hairy 1914-18 War blankets) to find a wee Glasgow 'keelie' by this time under the stallion's belly, who was standing stock still. When I asked what the hell he was up to, he replied, 'I've always wanted to be a Scots Grey! I wanted to mount this b——!' Strange how docile stock can be with those who are inebriated. Perhaps it is because the latter are relaxed, not tensed up and have no fear of the animal.

In the twenties a friend of my father, a Glasgow lawyer with more bawbees than had dad (an impecunious Church of Scotland minister) rented Machrie Water farm on the island of Arran. It was very usual in the years between the wars for farmers on the islands and up in the Highlands (Speyside is a typical example), if the farmhouse was fairly large, to vacate the house, let it and live in a wee tin hut at the back. It will seem strange to the younger generation of farmers today, but those two, or at best three, months' rent, would be one of the best, if not the best, cheques the farmer would receive in the whole year!

I can remember a time when an uncle of mine, who had made money in Canada, took a farmhouse in Kirkmichael, Perthshire, and kindly had me to stay. I immediately started working with the farmer. The highlight of that visit was a day at Blairgowrie Market with six greyface lambs which we put in an old box cart, with metal, not rubber wheels, the lambs kept in by an old fishing net draped over the top and the cart pulled by a cross-Clydesdale/Highland pony. As we left at 5 am I will never forget the farmer's wife's parting remark: 'Be sure and sell the lambs, else I'll

The incomparable 'Glenbruar'. 'Glenbruar' and 'Glenmuick' are to my mind the most impressive Highland ponies I have seen during the 65 years that I have been connected with the breed—the former because he was a brilliant sire, and the latter because he was my ideal Highland pony (John M. Macdonald)

have nothing with which to pay the monthly grocery bill!' And we had fourteen miles there and fourteen miles back! That's just how hard times were for farmers in the twenties.

But back to Arran, where as usual I worked on whatever farm would have me. Next to Machrie Water Farm, where we were staying, was Machrie Farm. Like most farms on that side of the island it was owned by the Duke of Montrose and tenanted by J.J. Morton, no farmer but full of good works. He was devoid of a sense of humour and a teetotaller (they often go together), an Elder of the wee Free Church, County Councillor etc. etc. His wife on the other hand was extremely practical and down to earth with a great twinkle in her eye, and was a daughter of Allan of Balnacoole. Mr Allan had owned the famous 'Lord Douglas', a stallion that had a tremendous influence on the Highland pony breed. Thanks to Mrs Morton I will probably be the only person alive today (at least at the time of writing!) to have seen the incomparable 'Glenbruar'. Old Morton was a modern Scrooge, the sort of farmer (and there are still some about) who thinks folding money is a halfpenny with a hinge in the middle! So Mrs Morton said to me, 'Ben, my friend Donald McKelvie, the grocer in Lamlash, employs boys in the summer, as he grows early potatoes and has a good stud of Highland ponies. I know you are horse-daft.' So it was that I was taken on by Donald McKelvie and in 1930 I saw the great horse who had to be put down the following year, when aged twenty nine, having sired three colt foals in his last season, all to be kept as stallions—Glenbruar, what a horse.

Then every holiday that my parents went to St Fillans I spent in Glenartney, the Earl of Ancaster's estate, where John (Shuachan) Ferguson was in charge not only of the estate but a stud of Highland ponies including many that had been bought in from the Islands through a Willie Tough of Stirling, a well known dealer in ponies in the thirties. The estate of Glenartney is widely famed from the poem that starts, 'In lone Glenartney's hazel shade,/ The stag at eve had drunk its fill'—famed that is to those who love poetry or the work of Walter Scott. But to sportsmen it was also known as one of the best grouse moors in South Perthshire. King George V shot there, and it is also the most southerly deer forest in Scotland and a good one at that.

Glenartney hired out no fewer than one hundred and forty ponies a season from Dumfries to Caithness, and there were others doing a similar job, but of them more later. All those ponies had to be handled before they went to their respective estates proven quiet. This was carried out down at the Comrie Railway Station, where there was a huge old wooden stable that had housed the railway horses. These railway horses had been used to distribute coal and other heavy goods to the manyestates around Comrie, but even in the thirties the internal combustion engine was taking over. I was one of many horse-daft laddies and lassies who helped ride the Glenartney ponies, chucking tins into panniers to get them used to noise, taking them to the bad-tempered old blacksmith to be shod, mostly for the first time—oh! just anything to get some riding free.

Then the great time came in 1935, when having been a grouse beater on the Lochside grouse moor above St Fillans, I was promoted to ponyman under Pat MacNab, who at eighty-five now is still hale and hearty. The next year, as Pat had taken a permanent job, I was promoted to the head ponyman's job.

So, dear reader, you can see why, when I came back from the war and was lucky enough to be appointed factor of different Highland estates and also have my own wee farms, I have continued to be more than a little interested in the breed. Since then I have done a stint on the Society's Council, and until I was eighty was on the judging panel.

One can only please one person when one judges, and so one makes more en-emies than friends. I always remember that great character, 'Bertie' Marshall of Cruggleton, of Shorthorn and Clydesdale fame, and a well-known and respected judge of both breeds. He was judging Shorthorns at an English show when the Chief Steward came up to him, saying, 'Mr Marshall, the judge of the Jack Russell terriers hasn't turned up, would you be good enough to stand in?' Bertie as usual was in 'pork-pie' hat, bow-tie and with pipe in mouth, which he just took out to say, 'I suppose I'll hae to do my best, all stock are the same. But I don't know their finer points.' Bertie then judged a vast class of some twenty terriers. When he had placed them, the owner of the second-placed dog came up to him and said, shaking his fist

in Bertie's face, 'My dog was first at Cruft's!' At this Bertie turned to the owner of
the dog with the red rosette, and enquired: 'Were you at Cruft's?' When the answer
was in the negative, Bernie said, 'Well, if you had been there, you'd have been first.'
He then asked, 'What do you think of my judging?' The reply, of course, was,
'Excellent!'—whereupon Bertie turned back to the second prize winner and said 'I
told you—two to one!' That's judging!

In the twenties and thirties mechanisation was already with us: it was everyone's
dream to own a car (nowadays nothing less than winning millions in the Lottery will
suffice). But at that time many crofts and small hill farms had their Highland pony as
the main source of transport and as a work horse in the real sense of the word. I first
learned to plough, in a rocky field beside Loch Earn (now covered with rushes),
with an ill-matched yoke of one Highland and one Clydesdale. The Highland pony,
called 'Kitty', was one of the most awkward pieces of horse flesh I've ever had to
handle, but no wonder, as she was expected to do everything on but the poorest of
rations. Her first job each day was to take the milk float, which carried a couple of
milk churns with taps attached, down the two miles to St Fillans. As it was another
mile and a bittock to go down to the main road bridge over the River Earn, Kitty
was tied to a fence opposite the foot bridge, on the far side of which was the
Drummond Arms Hotel in the middle of the village.

What I always remember about Kitty was that like most Highland ponies I've
handled she was perfectly docile when tied up, but could show quite a bit of mettle
when 'kittled' up, which as a harum scarum laddie I loved doing. I often wonder if
the milk wasn't sour by the time the villagers got it! They received it in milk cans
(pints or quarts) that they owned and had their own labels on the handles. The
handles were more than useful, as the person delivering the milk—me at certain
times of the year—rode an old-fashioned push bike with a lamp bracket on it, over
which we hung the milk can handles, and the milk got another good shake up!

What with the state of the byre in which the cows were milked, the muck on the
cows' udders, the lack of cleanliness of the hand-milkers' hands, the rusty state of the
churn, the condition of the cans and the way the milk was treated (it got sieved
through some muslin, which usually had some hay or dung left on it), considering all
these, shall we say, not exactly sterile things, a modern environmental health officer
would have a heart attack if he had visited that set-up. But there are still a lot of us
around who drank that milk, so it may be that we built up a few extra antibodies—
everything is so sterile and pasteurised today we don't seem able to fight off the
many bugs that beset us.

But back to Kitty. I had to drive her back up to the farm, 'house' (unyoke) her,
give her a wee feed of musty oats, and change her harness from trap harness to
working harness, with a stouter collar and a back band with chains, ready for her
place in the plough alongside the cross Highland Clydesdale. This I also had to
harness, and off I'd set on its back, as Kitty did not like being ridden. Kitty was
always wanting to be ahead of her 'other half', and I didn't realise until many years
later, when I ploughed with a decent well-matched pair of Clydesdales, what a

The Author, on his holidays, riding 'Blossom'

pleasure ploughing could be. With Kitty and her mate (I think his name was Charlie) I was never happy. First of all, I was inexperienced, and my tutor, the son of my boss, old Murdo Nicholson, had a habit of seeing to another job he was supposed to be doing and leaving me to it. Secondly, the field was so stony that all too often the plough 'stilts' (handles) would hit me on the chin when the plough hit a rock. Lastly, Kitty had a mind of her own, but for all that she taught me a lot.

Tuesday was market day in Crieff. Kitty was yoked to the ancient dog cart and, driven by old Murdo, took Mrs Nicholson the twelve miles there and back, or else to St Fillans Railway Station two miles away. Then, when the grouse shooting season came along in August/September, Kitty was leased out to carry panniers, much to Murdo's son's annoyance, as he reckoned she was needed on the farm. Times were hard and hard cash was not to be sneezed at, but I, like Murdo's son, was fed up that she was leased out for odd days, as it meant I had to do two or three runs per day on my bike from the farm to the village—an extra ten miles or so.

Though Kitty was the first Highland pony with which I worked, luckily there were to be many more that gave me more pleasure. There was 'Blossom', which Father kindly hired for me one summer because I had won the best recruit cup in the school O.T.C. (the only prize I ever won at school). I doubt if Blossom was pure Highland, her mouth was so tough she had no idea what a bridle and bit were for and so her brakes were non-existent; but she gave a teenage horse-daft laddie an awful lot of pleasure. Little did I realise how few 'bawbees' my Dad had to spare, and like many an offspring I took his gift as if it was my right. It wasn't until many, many years later I realised what he had sacrificed for his family.

There is a photo (reproduced here) of me riding Blossom wearing shorts instead of breeches, perish the thought, and with no hat, never mind a crash helmet. Blossom, as always, has her ears back, not enjoying the performance one bit—but I certainly did, and she taught me lots, but most of all how important proper breaking is. Sally, my wife, breaks a Highland pony every year, and spends weeks lunging and handling them. I would think that Blossom, like all the many ponies that went to the grouse moors and deer forests in the thirties, had all too little quiet breaking. These ponies of course landed up with mouths like iron, and all too often were unstoppable. God knows what they would have been like if they had been fed lots of oats!

Then there were those halcyon days when I was pony man on a grouse moor at St Fillans. I had to take four ponies from Woodhouse, on a Tuesday morning after Monday's shoot, to two miles 'Wast the village' (west of the village of Lochearn as described by the keeper Sandy Campbell) further up the loch to the Derry. This journey was repeated after a day's shooting, either to the Derry or, starting very early, to the other three grouse moors, Ardveich, Edinample and Ardvorlich. The last two were on the other side of the loch. The way it was done was by me riding the steadiest pony, tying another to its tail with a rope halter, leading the third pony from the ridden pony and having the fourth pony tied in turn to its tail. Today on that twisty road it would be completely impossible because of the cars one would meet and the speed at which they travel. As it was, docile as Highland ponies are, I had the odd trauma.

Talking of traumas, I'll never forget the time I volunteered to help Peter MacIntyre, head horseman at Glenartney and ex-rough riding Sergeant in the Scottish Horse, to take ponies to Dunblane Show. Because of the deer stalking there was an abundance of ponies in the glen, of which more later. Old John Ferguson, manager at Glenartney, had told the Secretary of the Dunblane Show that the Earl of Ancaster would be delighted to lend twelve ponies, all with saddles and bridles I might say, to the Show so that they could have a 'musical chairs' on horseback as one of the afternoon attractions. I'll bet the Earl never knew a blind thing about it, but Peter was told to get twelve ponies to the show.

Peter had four, I had four and A.N. Other the remaining four. We set off from Auchinner at the head of the Glen on the Friday, and got to Braco that night where the ponies were put in a field. After all those sixty-plus years I can't remember where we stayed, but I do remember being wakened at 'sparrow-fart' by Peter as he wanted to get down the road (now the dual carriageway A9) before the charabancs got going. Charabancs, for my younger readers (if any), were open-topped single-storied buses. They were very noisy, not only because of the engine, but also from the occupants, who were having their one day's outing in the year. When I drive down that stretch of road from Greenloaning to Dunblane I often have a wry smile on my face as I remember the scene as if it was yesterday. Young Coutts, who thought he was an accomplished horseman, was sitting astride his chosen mount, the one tailed

The ponies of 'lone Glenartney' (W.W. Weir)

behind was facing the wrong way, the two led ponies were over a dry stane dyke and running loose to boot and Peter was NOT amused. This had all happened because of one of the charabancs, the passengers in which we would now call 'yobboes' and who had probably never seen ponies in their lives before, started yelling when they saw us. The ponies, who had spent their lives in 'lone Glenartney', did not take kindly to this. In those days there were few people with money enough to take bus trips, but for some reason on that Saturday it seemed like the whole of Scotland was on that road.

However we got to the show in good time, and the sequel was that I won a rosette AND a bottle of ginger beer—big deal!—in the mounted musical chairs. Why? Because I knew the ponies, and made sure I got the one that stopped and started when I told it to.

In 1936 I went to Sussex to get a job, as there were none going north of the border for someone who had failed his veterinary exams as brilliantly as I had. I had been shepherding in Ettrick, but for no pay, just for my keep, and knew I could never compete with the Border 'herds' for the job they had learned from their fathers. They were steeped in their craft, and craft it is, but it will never be the same again. Although there are many notable exceptions, the advent of modern technology such as four-wheel drive motorbikes and TV has diminished the art: shepherds don't have time now to 'ken' their sheep as they used to because they have so many more to tend.

Even in the Borders there was interest in the Highland breeds, and among those well known to me before I headed down south there was one Border landlord who was a great Highland pony supporter, Sir Alfred Goodson—'Bill' to his friends. He made his shepherds use Highland ponies to gather their 'hefts' or 'hirsels', the units of the flock. Bill was a tremendous character: M.F.H. of the famous College Valley Foxhounds, and the breeder of some of the best foxhounds in the county, also of one of the top Aberdeen-Angus herds, as well as Border terriers, Cheviot sheep, you name it. I have more to say about this great stocksman in my chapter on ponies and cattle furth of Scotland.

Everything that Bill bred had its pedigree carefully sussed out, and he put pedigree and performance together and came out tops in all the breeds he owned. His famous line of 'Eulima' Aberdeen-Angus won many Highland shows. There's a lovely story told about him when he was out hunting his beloved College Valley Foxhounds. In the mounted field there was an extremely attractive blonde, who was attracting the attention of all the eligible males (and many who were not supposed to be eligible), and nearby was a foot-follower moving very easily behind the hounds, with the usual up-turned tackety boots, the hall-mark of a herd in the thirties, a tall, sparse, good-looking shepherd. Bill turned to his field-master and said, 'Isn't it a pity the master can't organise the mating of the field as he can his foxhounds—because those two would breed great stock'!

Dear Bill, you are greatly missed in many circles, and especially when it comes to breeding stock. You are missed by none more than the Highland pony breed, as you were before your time in breeding free-moving ponies—ones which are in such demand today, as more ponies are wanted for showing under saddle now than when you bred them. Bill Goodson—you may not have been bred in the Highlands, but you certainly loved all things Highland.

3

Highland Ponies between the Wars—Glenartney

As I was associated with Glenartney during the inter-war period, it seems to me to make sense that I start with that stud's involvement with the Highland pony breed in those days. There were over one hundred Highland ponies in the Glen at that time, and, more importantly, there were nineteen human families where today there are but two. Of the hundred Highland ponies, one can see by the photos that many were certainly not pure breds, but at least ten of the best mares were put to a pure Highland stallion. The man in charge of all the ponies, plus being the ploughman and the lorry driver, was Peter McIntyre of whom I wrote in the last chapter.

There was a famous 'Johnnie Copee', I think his name was Jock Smith, who travelled the Highland pony stallion. In his declining years he was asked what his best season had been, and he replied, in that lovely old-time Strathearn lilt: 'It would be back in 19 and 29, when we travelled Loch Tayside, and we had forty mares for the horses and fifteen for mysel'. The stallion men in those days had a great reputation for their 'way with the women-folk', which they were delighted to live up to!

Glenartney then would be renting out, at £1 per week for ten weeks, no less allowed, forty ponies to grouse moors and deer forests from Caithness to Dumfries. The mares had foals at foot. This meant that the foals learned to walk through burns, not jump them, as this would spell disaster were they loaded with panniers or a stag on their back. Not only that, they had to learn that those green moss areas, though lovely, are minefields for a pony.

Because of this necessary learning period for the foals the mares were kept in the glen, where eight riding ponies and four pannier ponies were needed each grouse-shooting day, plus two ponies that came out later with the lunch. The ponyman in charge of these two was in a very sought-after job, as he got to empty the bottles left over by the 'toffs' and seldom got home sober, however the ponies always saw that he got back safely. Looking back over the span of years, can you blame him? His wages would be £2 a week and whisky was 12/6d per bottle—over a quarter of his wages. Nowadays for doing the same job, though sadly using some vehicle or other rather than ponies, the ghillie will be getting £180 to £200 per week, with whisky at £10 to £13 per bottle. Thus the desire to polish off the bosses' unfinished bottles will not be so great, and in any case the post-war lunches on most grouse moors are not as splendid as they were. In fact I was on one shoot when the laird's wife thought the keepers' lunch looked much better than hers!

Well, after that digression, let's get back to the foals. These were all halter-broken, and I remember well helping Peter to do it. I use the same method here to this day. We have a long rope on the halter, which we take over the foal's back to the off (right-hand) side. When the foal takes off, as they invariably do, I give a firm jerk and land the foal, quite safely, on its back—they soon learn who is boss. Following this Peter used to tie his foal, as explained earlier, to a really quiet pony's tail, and before long the foal learned that it had to 'follow my leader'.

There was a wonderful moss at Braco where the large number of Glenartney ponies that were not needed after the summer were wintered out. A moss is a grand place for outwintering ponies, as it has a lot of roughness in the autumn, and the young rushes, or 'sprots' as they're called by hill men, come early in the spring and are much enjoyed by ponies. Highland cattle like them as well, whereas many other breeds wouldn't thank you for them no matter how hungry they were.

There was a lot of 'horse-dealing' in Glenartney. Peter MacIntyre, being so good at his job, and with his two paid and many unpaid assistants, would break dozens of ponies each summer. Some would be sold, to be replaced by ponies bought in the Islands by Willie Tough from Plean near Stirling. He would bring over anything from forty to fifty, some just halter-broken, but all too many unhandled. Comrie station was the ideal place for breaking ponies, with its old stable and a bothy beside it for Peter and his two paid helpers. There was a field where the ponies could get used to the old steam trains and a thriving village through which the ponies could be ridden, where there were not one, but two, blacksmiths.

Pat MacNab tells of the time he was sent down the glen with fifteen ponies all to be shod, seven to go to one blacksmith and eight to the other. Firstly, old 'Shauchan' Ferguson hadn't remembered, or conveniently forgot, that the stone-crusher was working full-blast halfway down the glen at Dalness. Poor Pat and his fifteen ponies got in 'one helluva fankle', but luckily in those days most men had had something to do with horses, so he got sorted out with help from some of the stone-crushing team at the Dalness quarry. Secondly, old Shauchan hadn't booked in his ponies, and one of the blacksmiths (MacNab, but no relation of Pat's) refused to shoe them. This left Jock Crerar, a crabbit old man at the best of times, with the task of shoeing fifteen previously unshod ponies. Some modern blacksmiths would think twice about facing even half a dozen unshod ponies one after the other, but Jock set to with the help of Pat, albeit after Pat had been despatched to the Royal Hotel for a bottle of 'the cratur' to help the Dutch courage.

When the ponies were being broken in at Comrie Station, they had to leave with a guarantee that they were docile in panniers—we used to throw empty cans into the panniers until the pony would stand still under a fusillade of them. Also they had to be rock steady when having a stag put on the deer saddle. Two stags were always shot in July, one in time for the 'milk clippings'—the clipping of the ewes with lambs at foot as opposed to the 'yeld clippings' in June, when the ewe hoggs, yearlings and the ewes without lambs were clipped. The other stag was sent to the station. They always had the heads taken off. I never knew why, unless it was to give the pony the smell of more blood, a thing they hate. Some stalkers to this day put a jacket over the pony's head, but I don't think it a good idea, as if you start doing it you have to do it forever, and Highland ponies can carry deer when they are in their twenties! Better by far to break them properly from the start.

As some deer forests demanded to have their ponies broken to dragging with chains, and others wanted a pony that would pull a cart, certain ponies were broken specifically for those jobs. What dedication Peter and his squad put into their work. What pleasure I know it gave Peter to see that the correct ponies went to the different estates. He would be in Comrie from May until August, staying in a bothy (which I know from personal experience was no five-star hotel) away from his family in the glen. What a relief it must have been to see anything up to forty to fifty ponies despatched in their twos, threes or fours to all parts of Scotland. Pat, who was his right hand man for two summers, thinks that Balquhidder was the furthest point that ponies were ridden to their destination, a good twenty-five miles!

To my mind what is sad about those so-called 'good old days' is that the Peters were never properly appreciated. Their wages were minute, but they never got a 'weel done, Jock' or that pat on the back we all appreciate when we think we've done a job well. Pat tells how his father was lured to Glenartney from the island of Eigg by Pat's uncle, who was at Tighnablair, on the Langside road between Comrie and Braco. Pat's father, Peter McNabb, whom it was my pleasure and privilege to know, came for the huge pay of thirty pounds per annum (!) plus the keep of an estate cow. As the cow's calf was by the estate bull, that calf had to go back to the estate after it was weaned. Having factored ten estates since 1945 I know only too well how some absentee landlords don't bother about their employees, and in all too many cases leave the employment of labour to the factor, but I think this is the meanest thing I've ever heard of, and especially to a man who was the salt of the earth.

I once had a day with him when he was training a dog called Bob, what an inspiration it was. He was top of his league in those days. That dog was sent to him because he had bitten someone, but by the time Peter had finished training him he could separate the 'tups' (rams) from the ewes at the end of 'tupping' time. And Peter was only worth £30 per annum! His dog training would make him a fortune today.

How they made ends meet baffles me. I know they used to get one boll oatmeal, ditto flour and one hundredweight sugar, plus seven pounds black twist pipe tobacco delivered at Comrie station from a Glasgow firm called Cochrane's, who were willing to wait until Peter was paid at the end of the year. Then, when I spent my blissful Christmas holidays with them in Staghorn Cottage, mother gave them the princely sum of £1 per week! In the summer they took in 'lodgers', and we all loved Peter and Katie so much we went back and back. But their like will be hard to come by again. Can you imagine a modern shepherd's wife walking the twelve miles from the glen down to Comrie on the day her husband was paid, to settle her account and to take home but a shilling or two? Certainly things got better for them in the late thirties, and I am only sad that after the war I didn't make more contact with them. Peter was looking after six hundred grazing cattle and five hundred ewes at the age of eighty-eight, and died aged ninety—so look out, Pat, you're heading for the Queen's telegram!

These are folk bred in the Highlands, and for various reasons the last of an era. But both the Peters, MacNab and MacIntyre, left sons who carried on working with Highland ponies and all things pertaining to the hills.

Pat MacNab, a robust eighty-five, is now retired in Comrie. He was my first boss as head pony man at St Fillans back in 1935, and will have done every job connected with hill farming, but loves to talk of his experiences with Peter MacIntyre making and breaking the Glenartney ponies. He also loves to regale us with the description of one of his winters spent in the Dubh Chroinn bothy as a rabbit trapper, when there were thousands of rabbits to be trapped. He got his rations once a week from Auchinner, the working headquarters of the estate at the head of Glenartney. The distance was six miles, and Pat says that before him a shepherd had lived there with his family, and the children walked to Glenartney School! What a tough race we were then: no wonder the Highland Regiments, folk bred in the Highlands, performed so well in two World Wars.

Pat had an amazing collie bitch, a real 'beardie' she was, called Mabel. When she was working with sheep she wouldn't look near a rabbit burrow, but when Pat went as a rabbit trapper in the winter she was transformed. She used literally to point with her tail at a burrow that housed a rabbit, but passed by all those which were empty! What ability! Lots of dogs had much more brain then than they have now, since as a country we have become obsessed with show points—or, in the case of collies, the 'one man and his dog' type of trial. In these trials the Mabels would score no points, but give me her kind any day. In situations when the dog has to work out of sight of its handler the modern collie would bring back one or two sheep, but the Mabels would bring back every sheep they could see. And woe betide that old ewe with lamb at foot stamping her front feet at the modern collie and getting away with it. The Mabels would shift them, and quickly too!

Alastair MacIntyre, Peter's son, has just retired as head keeper in Glenartney. He, very much one of the folk 'bred in the Highlands', remembers how much Highland ponies were part of the life of the Glen. Talking of the old days he wonders, as do many of us oldies, how his parents managed to bring up a family that was to be so successful. His sister, taken far too early with the dreaded cancer, was the youngest Hospital Matron in Scotland, some achievement. We agreed that luckily there was abundant free venison at certain times of the year. The Ruchil river then, but sadly not now, was full of salmon, and as my dear friend the late Johnnie (Lord) Bannerman used to say, 'Taking a salmon for the pot is not poaching'. And so say all of us. Alastair reckons his father lived for his Highland ponies, and was heartbroken when the Glen stallion, Ronald, was castrated at the age of twelve and sold to go down the mines of all places! How mean can people be?

Stalking at Glenartney (Polly Pullar)

It's interesting that between the wars stallions didn't have the prefixes of the stud on which they were bred, as I remember they had another stallion there then called 'Snowhope'. A fell stallion was introduced in the thirties, and other stud owners said this was because the Glenartney stud had a streak of 'quickness' in them. I find this hard to believe, as I worked with them for two and more years and found them, as Highland ponies were in those days, all too placid for a teenager who wanted to ride a Derby winner!

The ponies of Glenartney were one of a number of money-making activities in the Glen. The grouse shooting, on what was then one of the best moors in Central Scotland, was much sought after and commanded a big rent. During my days there in the thirties Mr Riley Smith, a Yorkshire brewer, was more than kind to us mere employees. He had a sectional dance floor made for the large garage and supplied a barrel of beer for our weekly dances, so as you can imagine he was hugely popular. The sale of venison would not come to much at that time. As a country we were not so worried then as we are today about the fatty foods we were eating, and the venison market was a small one, restricted to those who knew how good it can be when properly cooked.

In those days there were thousands of white mountain hares on the Ancaster-owned hills where there are but few today. It's strange that white hare and grouse numbers seem to ebb and flow together! The hares were shot in their hundreds around Christmas and New Year, and the shoots were organised by John Ferguson for his friends who had helped the Estate during the year. As hares run up to the top of a hill, unlike grouse and ptarmigan which stick to the contours, one didn't want to be the top gun, as one could end up with all too many hares to carry to the waiting ponies, and believe me they can be heavy brutes! The ponies had deer saddles on them: the hares had a slit made above the hock, and the long straps used to hold on a stag were slipped through and off went the pony back to the larder.

Those larders were always wonderfully positioned on the 'knowe', where it could get the benefit of all the winds that blow. To my dying day I'll never forgive myself for being a 'good boy' (unusual for Coutts) and obeying an E.E.C. directive that said that if an estate wanted to export venison it had to build a larder that resembled one of the gun emplacements you saw on the south coast during the last war! To the stalkers at Blackmount, the estate I was managing when I had this done, I must apologise for having you work in nothing like as pleasant conditions as your forebears. To the makers of those bloody silly directives from the E.E.C. (now the E.U.) my heartfelt curses upon you for knowing nothing about larders, or slaughter-houses for that matter.

I know not whether Scots as a race didn't eat game in the thirties (I've always loved it), but I do know that Peter MacIntyre had to set off every year to Manches-ter, of all places, in his ancient Ford lorry loaded with ice blocks, God knows where they came from, and hundreds of white hares.

There is no doubt that the blackfaced sheep would be one of the best money spinners for the Estate. Wool was in demand in those days. Sadly, it always needs a war for wool to make a price, and at that time World War II was imminent. Both Pat and Alastair tell of the famous day at the 'Are', on the other side of the Estate above Callander, when Fisher Ferguson, son of John and then manager, had organ-ised a gang of forty-six clippers, all clipping with hand shears, as electric clippers were unheard of then, and they clipped four thousand ewes in one day. Pat remem-bers it, as he was gathering one hirsel (roughly five hundred ewes) after another, and had only two hours sleep one night. Alastair, because he was 'crogging' (taking the sheep to the shearers), finished the day with no skin on his hands! My old friend 'Baldie' MacNaughton was then keeper at St Fillans and was brought over to pack the wool bags. He must have set up a record fit for the *Guinness Book of Records*, as he packed sixty-four bags. Wool bags then were over eight feet in height, and they were tied up to a cross-bar on a special framework. I, at six feet three inches, was out of sight in one.

What a day that must have been, and I only wish it had been recorded on film. These men were not only 'bred in the Highlands' but most, if not all of them were sons of shepherds, stalkers and keepers. Sadly this is no more the case, as fewer and fewer people are employed on estates, and everyone wants a higher standard of living. None of Pat or Alastair's families, who have all done well in their chosen occupations, have taken to the hill.

The end to the era of the great Glenartney pony stud came in 1939, at the outbreak of the war, when there was a special sale organised in Perth for the one hundred plus ponies. The average price was thirty pounds apiece, but Alastair says that although it was the only time he saw him with a tear in his eye, his father was thrilled that the pony he always rode, Betty, made the top price of eighty pounds. The main buyers were Norwegians, who wisely foresaw that petrol etc. would be scarce during the war and ponies could be fed off the land. I remember well in Glenartney pre-war how we would be out 'rucking' hay after a long day on the hill, as everything on four legs kept over the winter was fed on home-grown feed. Now not an acre is cropped, and all feeding is bought in. Sad, sad.

4
Ponies for All Seasons and Many Different Types of Work

In my chapter on Glenartney I touched on the jobs that Highland ponies were doing in the thirties: at that time they were mainly being broken to carry panniers for grouse or deer saddles for deer. Another famous stud, Gaick, owned by the Ormiston family and dating back to 1880, not only let out ponies to sporting estates, but after the Second World War started a highly successful trekking establishment. This was the brainchild of Ewan Ormiston, whose son, Cameron, now owns the stud. Ewan was born and brought up at Gaick, an estate which I was to manage in the fifties. Ewan's father had been head stalker there, and had always been keen on Highland ponies. He had used Atholl stallions. In his to-ing and fro-ing to Atholl, and just look up your map to see the distance and terrain over which he had to travel, he met the head housekeeper there whom he 'coorted' and married. When you think that from Gaick to Blair Atholl is over twenty miles as the crow flies, never mind the hills in between which rise to two thousand six hundred feet plus, and the fact that they are snow-covered for more than four months in the year, I say again they were special folk, the folk bred in the Highlands.

Gaick is the only estate that I've managed that had the original Water Closet. It was a beautifully built wee stone house built over a swift-flowing burn, but what intrigued me was that it had a double seater inside! I think one would have to know the other person terribly well to want to share the loo for 'one's duties we have to do each day', to quote a hymn out of context. It was bad enough in the war when many of us had dysentery, and there were slit trenches dug with a pole resembling a perch in a hen house on which we sat. And to quote an old army joke, 'What's the difference between the cemetery and the lavatory?' 'None, when you've got to go you've got to go.' Then one couldn't be fussy who one sat beside.

But to the nicer things about Gaick. Had I ever made enough money to buy and run a non-viable estate, Gaick is the one I would have chosen. It's the old story of the 'burn heid', as the Border sheepmen say, in other words that its situation at the top of the burn/river means that the goodness has not been washed out of it. Gaick in the fifties was the reservoir for the grouse stock on Glentromie which is the estate below it and then well known as a grouse moor. Gaick as a deer forest had the tremendous advantage that it had two good pony paths on to the stalking beats, one to the east and one to the west. This meant that the wind, which is usually one or the

'Ebony Polly of Croila' at Blair Atholl (Ruaridh Ormiston)

other, could be gauged in the morning and one could set off along the path heading into the wind. One does this so that the deer can't get wind of you, as not only do they have fantastic eyesight but a very highly developed sense of smell.

Then there is the lovely wee Loch-an-Seilich right beside the Lodge which has, or had, good trout fishing and in the autumn the odd salmon. There's a lovely story told about one of the stalkers who succeeded old Ormiston. The estate was then owned by the MacPherson-Grants, who had it until the fifties when it was bought by the Hone family for whom I factored it. The MacPherson-Grants allowed their relations to fish the loch. One such was a regular fisherman, but never gave the stalker a tip or a dram and the stalker spent many hours rowing the boat for this character. On this occasion the person in question landed a better than average salmon and was so excited when he was trying to weigh it on the old spring scales we used to use, he had forgotten his spectacles. He said to the stalker, 'Pass me my glasses.' Back came the reply from his fed-up companion: 'To hell with the glasses, where's the bottle?'

When I took on the factorship of Gaick in the fifties the Ormiston influence was still much to the fore. And so it should be, as old Edward (I can't think how that name came into a family, the rest of whom have super Scottish names like Ewan, Cameron, Rhuaridh, Fergie and Dochie—Duncan to the sassenachs) did something that would be impossible today, when he took the good black Highland mare 'Mountain Polly' to the Paisley Highland Show in 1911 and won the overall Championship. Why I say no one will do that feat again is that the mare was walked from Gaick to Kingussie, fourteen miles, then put in a cattle truck, which was shunted at least twice, won the Championship and went back to Gaick to perform her usual duties as a deer pony. I'm afraid our modern pampered Breed Champions would not enjoy that sort of treatment. I am only sad that history didn't repeat itself—in 1989 Edward Ormiston's grandson, Cameron, showed a black mare of the same breeding, 'Ebony Polly of Croilla', all those years later, that was female Champion, but which many round the ring thought could have been overall Champion.

When Ewan was a lad in Gaick their only transport was a cart, which had to be sturdily sprung because of the gravel road, and was pulled by a Highland pony. Their nearest neighbour was five miles away at Braan, and they had no telephone, wireless or TV, but my goodness they learnt so much about nature and the hills. It comes as no surprise to me that Ewan earned a Military Medal in the First World War. But just imagine his annoyance on his return when he applied for the stalker's job at Gaick to be told that he was too young and inexperienced! As was the case with many another, myself included, it may have been a blessing in disguise, as he vowed he wouldn't put in for another stalker's job, trained in the butchery trade, and by the time I knew him in the fifties he not only owned the butcher's shop in Newtonmore but also the Balavil Hotel, and then the highly successful trekking business which at the height of its popularity used no fewer than two hundred Highland ponies. Before I met Ewan, who was a most engaging character, he had been training commandos in hill craft and had met all the top deer-forest owners in the Highlands. Some were to be his friends to his dying day, but there were some who looked on him as a poacher, as he took many deer forests during the Second World War and culled them severely, which they were certainly needing. As I always say, 'You're no doing any good till they're all agin' you.' And if they all like you, look out! I remember in 1952 one could have an Easter Holiday week at the Balavil Hotel, with trekking through some of the most lovely scenery in Scotland, for twelve and a half guineas, those were the days! What's more there were no grants from Scottish councils, Highland Development Boards etc. at that time.

Cameron carried on where his father left off and still has eighty ponies of which twelve are brood mares. Trekking sadly is not as popular in Scotland as it was, as people nowadays have more money to spend on holidays and leisure, and can go to America, Spain, Portugal, France, you name it, and can trek with the bonus of sunshine (but not the Highland scenery, which is second to none). After taking over the Gaick stud Cameron gave the prefix Gaick to Dochie and for a time took Glentromie as his own prefix. With 'Glentromie Trooper' he won the Championship at the Highland Show, and then went on to Olympia where he won the Mountain and Moorland Championship.

The Ormiston dynasty goes from strength to strength, as not only has Dochy got Gaick as a prefix but Rhuraidh has Creag Dhu (the hill overlooking Newtonmore).

Fergie is doing more than well with Highland cattle, and had an outstanding cow at the Highland Show in 1995 which was reserve overall Champion. Cameron has now switched his prefix to Croila, a hill opposite Kingussie, which he says resembles a horse. Since the early days of exporting ponies to Europe the Ormistons have been involved, and Cameron remembers the first three that went to Hamburg being loaded into wooden crates at Leith docks for shipment.

Another who is very much involved in the export trade is Scott McGregor, whose father Hugh, like Cameron's, was much involved in the pony-trekking era of the fifties and sixties. Hugh actually started his trekking centres in 1953 and he and Scott ran five centres when that kind of holiday was at its peak. They were as widely scattered as it was possible to manage from their farm at Thornhill, which was near the main centre at Aberfoyle. Elsewhere they had a centre in the Trossachs, another in Glen Devon in the Ochil Hills, and two in England, one in the Peak District and the last at Windermere, where they had a tie-up with a hotel group.

It's interesting today to compare horse trekking with all the other forms of out-door recreation. There is a surge of townees wanting to use the hills walking, climbing, skiing etc., and in all too many cases they are spoiling the very thing they want to enjoy, i.e. the hills and the environment, especially with the rubbish they leave, but the horse trekkers stick to tracks, all stop for their meal together at one place and so pick up their rubbish. But most important of all they don't disturb stock. You can ride almost up to a herd of red deer before they move, but try to do it on foot. One of the things that annoyed me most in my factoring days was the few walkers who spoil it for the many, by wandering (in highly coloured apparel) onto grouse, deer and sheep land, clearing all before them. Although they have been warned where not to go at certain times of the year, they seem to think the hills belong to them. I wonder if they would like to pay the rates and the estate upkeep? But pony-trekkers, to which recreation Highland ponies have contributed so much, are far more con-trollable. And where better to see our wonderful Highland scenery from, than the back of a Highland pony? At the height of their trekking operation the McGregors were using one hundred and sixty ponies.

The McGregors were among the few Highland pony enthusiasts just after the Second World War who were working their ponies: all too many just kept them to show or to breed from, enjoying the sight of a foal gambolling in their paddock. As a pal of mine said, 'They might as well keep, breed and show canaries and it would be cheaper.' One of the stallions that did a lot of good at Ballinton was 'Merlin of Derculich', but before that they had bought 'Ledi Hiker' from the late Jack Cameron for the vast sum of thirty-two pounds!

Jack was of hill stock, and to my mind was one of the best that I've seen at showing a Highland pony. He was always turned out spick and span and wearing riding breeches, and really lifted his knees up, which is most impressive for the judge. However, when selling sheep from his farm of Glenfinglas he was completely differently attired, as (although Chairman of Livestock Marts in Stirling) he would come into the ring wearing a filthy old mac tied in the middle with binder twine,

'Trigger' with Hugh McGregor aboard. This pony was not only Hugh's favourite, but was an exceptionally good riding pony and won many ridden class championships (Scott and Maryanne McGregor)

and splashed all over with stains of an oil we then used to eradicate liver-fluke in sheep. The disguise didn't fool those of us who knew that not only was he Chairman of the Mart, but also farmed Balbuthie, an excellent arable farm in Fife, but it must have fooled the English buyers judging by the prices Jack got for his stock, which I must say were excellent.

'Trigger' was Hugh McGregor's favourite trekking pony. He was one of the first Highland ponies that Hugh bought. Like many who went into the breed post-war, Hugh was a Clydesdale enthusiast, and when 'Windsordene', a Clydesdale, was the travelling stallion in the Logiealmond karea, he was stabled at Willie Simpson's at Chapelhill. Today Chapelhill is famous for the successes they have had in the show ring. One year at the R.H.A.S. they not only had the in-hand champion but had bred the ridden champion, some going. For all that, I remember best of all the times when I danced to the young Willie's superb fiddle playing, especially when the tune was 'The Duke of Perth'. At any rate, this is what led to Hugh buying 'Trigger'. It seems Willie Simpson senior had bought 'Trigger' at a horse sale in Perth, little realising that he was a pure-bred Highland pony bred at Kinimouth by Heather Gow's father. He must have been a super riding pony, as he won the ridden mountain pony championship at the Highland Show more than once in the days before each breed had its own ridden section. Although pedigreed, it was called 'Trigger' after one of the horses in a Wild West film. These were all the rage after the war before the advent of the 'Telly'.

Because of the fact that Hugh and Scott were interested in working their ponies, Scott had to break on an average twenty-five a year, which means he has broken some six hundred and fifty in his time—quite a record. The stud's latest success has been 'Falcon Frost of Sauchrie', which has won just about everything he could, although the Olympia Championship eluded him (though many ringside judges thought he should have won). 'Falcon Frost' is now in Germany where there is a big demand for Highland ponies, but of that later.

Then of course when one thinks of the Highland ponies working, one has to remember their great contribution to the two Highland Yeomanry Regiments, the Scottish Horse and the Lovat Scouts. Sadly, between the two wars the horses for the annual camps of the Scottish Horse were a mixed bunch, supplied by the Barries from Glasgow, and a rough lot they were, as I know to my cost. After the Scottish Horse camps the horses were moved on to other annual camps of mounted Territorials/Officers Training Corps, and I was in the latter as a veterinary student. Luckily for me I knew Jack Barrie, who tipped me off as to which was the best horse in the lot, and on it I won the mounted games at camp in Blair Atholl of all places.

Little did I realise, back in 1935, that I would lease a leg in a racehorse with the 10th Duke of Atholl, be Agricultural Adviser to a TV show called 'Strathblair', filmed in the Blair Atholl area on my suggestion, and most importantly, from a Highland pony point of view, start a working Highland pony class which is judged annually in front of Blair Castle. But 'Tempus Fugit'. Highland ponies may not have been as pure-bred and pedigreed as we know the breed now in the nineties, but the Scottish Horse and Lovat Scouts certainly thought highly of them, and they were what they used as mounts between the two World Wars.

The late Colonel 'Bobbie' Campbell-Preston of the Scottish Horse tells a story of a regimental occasion in Edinburgh in the twenties, when the Scottish Horse were being reviewed by the King. The Colonel was, of course, the then Duke of Atholl, and as he was about to ride past the saluting dias his medals became detached and flew off his chest. Luckily they went in the direction of his A.D.C., who caught them brilliantly, and as Bobbie says, 'He should have been picked for the English Cricket XI immediately to field in the slips.'

Major Michael Leslie Melville has written an excellent book called *The Story of the Lovat Scouts 1900-1980* in which there are many references to that regiment's use of Highland ponies. The late Colonel Ian Grant of Rothiemurchus was a close friend of mine in my Gaskbeg days over forty years ago, and like me he enjoyed 'a tellin of the tale'. It seems that Iain had been detailed, with the regular Sergeant Major (which every Territorial regiment had posted to them between the two wars) to see the men of the famously bibulous 'B' Squadron, which was recruited from the Islands, back to their respective islands after annual camp. You can well imagine the scene, with a crowd of lads who have had that wonderful camaraderie that only

Highland ponies were used by the Royal Army Veterinary Corps during the 1939-45 war and also later because of their ability to adapt to difficult terrain as shown here (Lieutenant Colonel P.A. Roffey D.L., RAVC)

comes when one is in the services. They were going home to face the hard life that was theirs pre-war on the Islands no matter what their occupation was. They wouldn't be meeting together for another year and, having just sold their ponies at enhanced prices, they had money in their pockets just waiting to be spent. Of course, having come from the wet windy climate of the Western Isles, they thought there was only one way to spend it, on that famous antidote to the weather, whisky.

The result was mayhem for 'Iain Og' and his Sergeant-Major. He, in typically regular Sergeant-Major style, as the ship came to an island and a rowing boat came alongside (there were but few piers in those days) shouted 'Ten off here, Sir,' or 'Sixteen', or whatever number had enlisted from that island. As far as the Sergeant-Major was concerned it didn't matter one iota whether the trooper (or in all too many cases the comatose body) belonged to that island or not, just as long as his numbers were correct in the book which he had to return to Headquarters. As ferries then were few and far between I shudder to think of the chaos this caused to the crofting communities all those years ago.

After the First World War, in fact it was 1922, the Lovat Scouts numbered some four hundred Territorials. To save money the then War Office said that only one in four should have a pony, and the other three were to have bicycles—we were as mean in our defence spending then as we are in the nineties! However by 1935 the Scouts were to become fully mounted as a mobile unit ready to scout and reconnoitre. A Cavalry General who came to inspect the Scouts at their annual camp was impressed with their ponies, about which he wrote: 'Although small for normal Cavalry work they are ideal for the role for which the unit is being trained.'

On mobilisation for the Second World War no fewer than eighty ponies had to be shipped to the mainland, along with their tack and, of course, their owners, which was some undertaking for Lt Simon MacDonald of Largie, Mull of Kintyre, who was in charge of the operation. Simon's account of how he had to take all the Army saddles, bridles, surcingles, etc., plus the calling up papers for eighty men is most amusing. When he eventually got them to Lochboisdale the requisitioned boat, owned by who else but MacBrayne, was hours late in arriving. The lads were having a whale of a time in the local hostelry until eventually that most genial of Highland hoteliers said enough is enough and closed the bar. I would guess, knowing Findlay MacKenzie in later years, the lads had drunk his pub dry! I was to meet Simon many years later and could well imagine he was more than up to his job. When the Scouts went to Lincolnshire to join a Cavalry Division, before horses were abandoned, quite rightly, in favour of mechanised units, the Division held a point-to-point meeting. Naturally the Highland ponies were not up to that, but not to be outdone, 'A' Troop, all mounted on dun Highland ponies, turned out and paraded, much as foxhounds do at today's National Hunt meetings, and were greatly admired by the knowledgeable horse-cavalry officers.

One very well-known judge of horseflesh said how much he admired the ponies, that were fourteen and a half hands at the most but were carrying eighteen stone at least! That was back in 1940, and yet there is a strong body of opinion in the nineties that would like to see the ponies bigger. For me big was never beautiful for the ponies, cattle or sheep that have to live off the sparse keep we have in the Highlands. Come to think of it, some of the best fighting troops I ever saw were Cockneys, Glaswegians, wee Northumbrian miners and of course the Ghurkas, all of whom were small. And I still might have my own nose had I not been six foot three inches tall! Highland ponies have contributed a lot to their native country in the past, so let's look at some of the folk and areas that evolved the breed.

5
Ponies and Their Background in Mull

Since the last war I have had a love affair with Mull. My family used to pull my leg about this until they visited the island and also fell under its spell. The strange thing is I can't put a finger on my reason for liking it more than the other islands on which I have judged stock or bought stock or just went to spend a holiday. It may be because apart from family holidays in Arran, Mull was the first island on which I spent time and had a job to do, so I got to know the people and their problems and their love of the real joys of life: tending their stock, pursuing old crafts like stick making (which is being carried on to this day by the famous Campbell family), enjoying ceilidhs, and just living a normal stress-free existence which has now sadly gone thanks to the super new roll-on roll-off ferry, *The Isle of Mull*. In one day in 1995 it took no fewer than one thousand cars over. This has transformed the island, which is now a gold mine for those catering for the 'Towerists'. So what's new? This country has made money its God, so good luck to it.

As an 'oldie', however, I recall the days of the *Lochinvar* with that super skipper Calum Black, who, like all sea-going islanders, yearned to farm when he retired, and so was more than kind to me in those far-off fifties when I was broadcasting on farming matters twice a week, and also advising on three estates on Mull. I think I'm right in saying the *Lochinvar* carried four to six cars, that were perilously driven off over two planks on their arrival at whatever pier was their destination. I do know for certain that on one occasion at Craignure, where the hundreds of cars and buses are now off-loaded, the late Lord Macleod of Fuinary, the founder of the Iona Community, and yours truly were the only two in the rowing boat that took us ashore because the tide was too far out to berth at the pier.

The reason I was there was that during the war serving in the Sussex Yeomanry my best friend was a Tom Mann, whose cousin Elizabeth was married to Sir Charles Maclean of Duart (later to be my vice-president of the Highland Cattle Society and, as Lord Maclean, Chamberlain to the Queen). 'Chips', as Sir Charles was known, asked me to advise him on his hopelessly non-viable estate of Duart. Through Chips I was introduced to the Rankins, who had that lovely estate on the west of Mull which included the Tresnish Islands (now used as a tourist attraction to observe seals, which to my mind eat far too much of our precious fish!) and the De Klees Estate of Auchacraig, one of the loveliest estates (and viable to boot), that I've ever been connected with. Then there was Glengorm, now famous for its Highland cattle fold, but just after the war owned by a Dr Dick Fawcett. Mull just post-war was infamous as being owned by 'Mad Majors and Dotty Doctors' and Dick was certainly one of the latter. Glengorm House looks out over the Atlantic, and I think there will be nothing between it and America. I will never forget spending a night there when (a) Dick informed me that gin and whisky were in short supply and that he needed it all for himself and (b) I was so cold I had to take up the carpet from the floor to cover my bed clothes!

Another occasion with Dick that will go down in the Coutts' history books under the heading of 'Mull Estates Advisory Work' was when I was due to go out to Mull after the Highland Cattle Bull Sales i.e. mid-February. I was to meet Dick at the then Station Hotel, Oban, now named the Caledonian. It was blowing a force eight gale, and we got word from Calum that he might not sail, but if he was going to he would blow the siren. Dick and I had the 'weakness' (that well known phrase in the Highlands) for enjoying a fair amount of drink, and had all too many thinking that Calum wouldn't be sailing. Our lovely reverie was broken when Alec, the doorman (and sadly they don't breed his sort any more) burst into the bar and said, 'Chentlemen, did you not hear Calum calling you?' Dick and I were the only passengers on board that night, and the *Lochinvar* was infamous for rolling at forty-five degrees, but Dick and I were anaesthetised! Infamous that lovely old ship may have been for being unstable, but by gosh! she served the best breakfasts I've ever eaten.

During those Mull visits I was to hear of the influence the Calgary Stud had on the Highland pony breed, and also that of the Tiroran (pronounced Chiroran, I found) Stud. I was to meet Brigadier Cheape of Tiroran in the fifties because he had a fold of Highland cattle. I never saw him dressed in anything but khaki shorts even at the February Bull Sales in Oban! My lasting memory of him dates back to the fifties when I was farming a high (one thousand feet above sea level) farm in upper Speyside, at a time when every halfpenny was hard to come by. I was in Oban with some old cast Highland cows (in their teens) and had a captive buyer from Yorkshire sitting beside me to whom I was saying how docile they were etc. etc., when suddenly I saw the Brigadier on the other side of the Yorkshire man. By then he was, as we oldies say, 'slightly deaf in one ear', which actually means you've got to bellow! So I shouted, 'Brig., I was just telling this Yorkshire farmer how quiet old Highland cows can be, wouldn't you agree?' Back came the reply: 'Mine are so bloody wild I take the Elephant Gun to them!' End of Coutts' deal with Yorkshire Farmer!

But it was through my meetings with the Brigadier that I got to know Bruce, his son, who was able to fill me in on the impact that Tiroran had on the Highland pony scene. It may be apocryphal, but it is said that when Bruce was eventually released, having been a prisoner of war for four years and got back to Mull, instead of giving him a hero's welcome, the old Brigadier said, 'No Cheape is taken prisoner, they shoot themselves first.' And knowing the crusty old man as I did, I can well believe it.

That great sire 'Rory of the Hills' was purchased by one of Angus's forebears,

Talisker House. On this estate the famous 'Rory o' the Hills' was bred, who did so much good to the breed in Mull

and was used extensively in Mull where he had a tremendous influence on the future of the breed. The forebear in question, of course, was 'The Squire', as Bruce's grandmother was known, and what I have heard of her makes me realise where the 'Brig', dressed in his tattered khaki shorts, got his toughness from! The original mares at Tiroran were from Atholl, and were brought from the Atholl Stud in 1891 along with a stallion 'Glascorrie Laddie', which John MacDonald doesn't mention in his excellent book. For the original money to buy and live in Tiroran—and believe me, if one wanted to live in Mull 'in the manner to which one was accustomed' on the mainland in the early part of this century, in fact up to the seventies, one had to have considerable other assets—the Cheapes had to thank a forebear who manufactured pins and needles in Redditch! Except for midge bites in Mull I can't see that the island has much else in common with pins and needles!

As with all successful studs, there was a faithful employee who helped The Squire. The same happens to this day, and I see them at shows and race meetings and three-day events, those people in the background who make a stud or trainer's yard tick. In the case of Tiroran it was 'Baldie Mhor'. To those of my English readers, if I have any, Baldie refers not to the person's lack of hair, but is the abbreviation of Archibald, and 'mhor' means big in the Gaelic whereas 'beag' is small. Baldie was like many in the islands today, dependant on two jobs to make a living. Three days a week he was the roadman, long before tarmac, and had a wheelbarrow, a brush and a shovel, all necessary on those old gravel roads I remember so well. The local saying was, 'what goes up and down the road but never touches it?' Answer, Baldie's shovel! But like many of his kind Baldie was super with the ponies and he worked the other three days at Tiroran. The thought of working on the Sabbath was anathema to all Highlanders then, whereas now most horse shows seem to be on a Sunday.

The Squire, as I've said, was very forthright and stated how she reckoned a Highland pony should be built. Interestingly enough she wanted the size to be up to fifteen hands, a matter on which as I've stated in a former chapter the present Highland Pony Society Council are divided. But what did interest me from the records Bruce produced for me was how she couldn't thole a 'ewe neck' in a pony (to the uninitiated a scrawny neck), as it is one thing I can't stand either. I love that bold crest Highland ponies should have, with that wonderful flowing mane, the envy of all other mountain and moorland breeds.

The Squire must have been some lady, as she set off to Uist in 1894 on the SS Flowerdale which very nearly foundered in one of those sudden storms that they can get off the Western Isles. There is the well-known story of the famous skipper on the MacBrayne's boats who was known as 'Squeaky Robertson' because of his high-pitched voice. Sailing to Lochboisdale one day he hit one of those force nine gales which (in the days before radar, up-to-date weather forecasting etc.) could suddenly hit a vessel. Hours after the official landing time 'Squeaky' berthed his ship, and as he was doing so an old lady (who had been ghastly sick) came on the bridge and said, 'Thanks to you, Captain Robertson, and the Lord, we've made land.' Whereupon Squeaky, in his high-pitched voice, replied 'Two good men!'

It would not be 'Squeaky' who was in charge when The Squire went to Uist, but whoever it was had told the islanders that 'a lady from Mull' was coming with a possibility of buying a pony or two. Imagine her astonishment when she arrived at Lochboisdale to find dozens of ponies on the pier. But we now live in an affluent age, and judging by the trolleys I see in the supermarkets piled high with junk food, no one is as hard up as the Uist crofters were, so we shouldn't wonder they brought their ponies to the pier and were willing to wait for hours, perhaps a day, for a possible buyer who would actually give them cash in their hand for their pony. To me the most interesting part of this famous excursion by The Squire was that three of four of those Highland ponies landed up as hunt horses at the Bentley Hunt, to which my informant about the Tiroran Stud, Bruce, was a whipper-in. I think one of the best things that The Squire left (apart from her family) was the knowledge she built up that crossing Highland pony mares with a Clydesdale was a disaster, and if one had to cross them it should be with a Cleveland Bay or a thoroughbred—and that brings me on to the other stud in Mull that had such a dramatic effect on the future of the Highland pony breed.

I, having been lucky enough, because of my varied career, to have travelled almost world wide, have no doubts that my favourite view in the world is from Calgary Castle looking out over those fabulous white sands. The view, I might say, is greatly helped by a large dram from the custodian, one Adam Brown, who looks after it for the present owner, a Frenchman who has made his money in making ladies even more attractive by manufacturing scent! But for Highland pony breeders the name of Calgary means Highland ponies of what was known as the 'Island' type. J H Munro Mackenzie reigned supreme in his day in advocating that the Highland ponies which had been employed for years up to then as work horses, on crofts or as deer or pannier ponies, should be used as riding ponies, and that they should be bred with more action than the super docile plodding 'garron' type used on the crofts.

The result was that the Highland Show had to split their classes between the mainland type, which were used for work on the croft, and the Island type, which Calgary had devised as suitable for riding. This division continued until the winners of both sections were by the same sire! Munro Mackenzie was not only a fanatical Highland pony breeder but 'a Great Scot'. He was on the Parochial Board, the District Committee, the Parish Council and the Poorhouse Committee, plus being a Justice of the Peace. For all those jobs he never got one penny in expenses, although he reckoned he had ridden on his Highland ponies six thousand miles *pro bono publico* during his years of good works. On one occasion he rode from Calgary to Auchnacraig and back!—and then Oban to Ardrishaig and back, a distance of sixty-three miles, which makes modern councillors, of which I was one for four years, look pretty poor mortals! To this day there are breeders of Highland ponies who blame Calgary for getting away from the traditional garron type, but those who wish to ride, event, drive or use their ponies for recreation rather than hill or croft work, have a lot to thank him for—especially for, as he said himself, 'Getting better shoulders, withers, backs and action into these hardy ponies.' He it was who sold the good stallion 'Skerryvore' to Edward VII which won the Highland Show on three occasions, once for King Edward and twice for King George V. Apart from his passion for Highland ponies and setting up a riding type that exists to this day he was a brilliant shot, and one day when the woodcock flighted into Calgary in a frosty spell he shot one hundred and twenty to his own gun. I wonder if Adam who now looks after 'the big hoose' and surrounding woods, as the estate is now split up, sees more than twenty these days during a frosty spell! See the wonderful photo on the next page, from the *Oban Times* dated June 22nd, 1935, of J H Munro Mackenzie OBE (which he had been awarded in World War I as chief coast watcher on Mull) and Mrs Mackenzie on the celebration of their Diamond Wedding, with himself driving a pair of Highland ponies, both of which had been Reserve Champions at the Highland Show.

For those of us who have bred stock all our lives 'a great breeder' means a stallion, bull, boar or ram that stamps its progeny with certain attributes. I know in this modern age people don't seem to realise how much part genes play in how one reacts to life, but one of my sons who has scoffed at my belief in genes has come to realise that his father isn't as scatty as he thought, after we discussed a mutual friend who had adopted two children, knowing nothing of their parents' background, and then wondered why she was having problems!

The reason I am bringing this in is because the great Munro Mackenzie had a daughter Norah, later to become Lady Fairfax-Lucy, who was a Highland pony fanatic, not just an enthusiast. Oh! I know there are many of 'the old and the bold'

J. H. Munro Mackenzie O.B.E. at the front of Calgary Castle, with a pair of Highland ponies he used regularly to transport him to his many committees (Mrs Bartholemew)

in the breed who didn't agree with her, but there's an old Scottish saying I've already quoted, 'You're no doin' any guid till they're all agin' ye'. Or to put it another way, watch out for those who scratch your back!

Lady Norah Fairfax-Lucy was the youngest of Munro Mackenzie's eight children, and all her life—and she died at the age of eighty-six—she was to devote herself to the Highland pony breed. Although she had qualified in Horticulture at Reading University she decided to start a riding school at Rickmansworth where she used Highland ponies. Sadly her marriage to Sir Henry Fairfax-Lucy in 1944 was a short one, as he died soon after they were married. As there were no children, she immersed herself in everything to do with ponies, naturally mainly Highland ponies, and she sat for many years on the Highland Pony Council. She was President in the present Queen's Coronation year, and on behalf of the Society presented HM with 'Norah of Meggernie' (the name was sheer coincidence, as the mare was bred by Sir Earnest Wills of Meggernie.) But Milady Norah not only backed up her own breed but was a Councillor of the National Pony Society for many years, just as her father had been before her at the turn of the century.

She introduced Highland ponies to the south west of England, and like many another reckoned that 'no good pony is a bad colour'. Sadly the Highland Pony Society didn't agree, but of that more in a later chapter. Altogether Lady Norah was a larger than life character like her father before her. But 'Calgary' stamped his genes not only on Lady Fairfax-Lucy but also on his son's daughter Kirsty.

Kirsty was the daughter of Commander Kenneth Mackenzie, and after she had seen service in the WRNS (as a radio mechanic of all things, as she said) she became devoted like her grandfather to Highland ponies. Kirsty must have been one of those few whom horses trusted, as the story is told by Audrey Holmes of the time back in the days of the *Lochinvar* which took cattle, sheep and ponies from Mull to the mainland, that Kirsty had handled an eight-year-old Highland pony mare that had never been haltered, far less broken! The mare was called Lizzie, and was one of six going from Mull to Kirsty's pony-trekking establishment at Ardfern twenty-three miles south of Oban. The ponies had to be at Tobermory at 7 am, because by the time the *Lochinvar* got to Salen the tide would be wrong to get the ponies on board. So they set off from Calgary with four of the six, three ridden and one led. Calgary to Salen is seventeen miles. At Salen they picked up 'Lizzie', the eight-year-old, and another, Morag (a nice change in names from Polly, which was very popular in the islands after shipwreck of the *SS Politician* and its load of whisky, immortalised by Compton Mackenzie in *Whisky Galore*). It took two men to saddle Lizzie, but Kirsty got on board and got her to Tobermory, she must have been some horsewoman. Then it was Kirsty who would be one of the few, if not the only person, to get a stallion into a rowing boat to get it ashore to one of the outer isles—most people would have made it swim behind the boat. And it was Kirsty who, having worked in a horse-dealer's yard for five years in Canada, sent thirteen ponies from her Ardfern Stud to Canada, and they went right out west to British Columbia. This was by far the largest consignment of Highland ponies up to then, the year being 1953. Now there is a tremendous interest in Europe in all our native pony breeds, as they have virtually no pony breeds as such, but at that time, although this country was called 'the stud farm of the world' and cattle, sheep and Clydesdale horses were exported to North and South America in their hundreds, there were no pony exports.

Kirsty's exports included a two-year-old stallion, Islesman III, and the Canadian ordered thirteen all told. As there were no repeat orders I wonder if Kirsty shouldn't have sent another as a 'luckspenny', since thirteen was never a lucky number.

In this affluent age when most houses have a car, and many have two, the holiday-makers who go to Mull enjoy its tarmac roads although most are single track with passing places. Those passing places are horrendous for the English 'Towerists' towing a caravan, who are used to driving on motorways and without a clue as to how to back that caravan. But it was not always thus, as in the days up to and just after the last war many roads were gravel. There is a lovely road like that up the west coast of Mull to this day, very twisty and narrow and with narrow bridges. From Tiroran to Salen, the nearest pier to which the *Lochinvar* used to call once a day, is some twenty miles. On one occasion the faithful Baldie Mhor was despatched to collect a very special guest to Tiroran and instructed to look after him particularly well. Unfortunately, because of fog, the *Lochinvar* was delayed, and Baldie, like any good Highlander, made for the nearest port of call, the Salen Hotel. As the *Lochinvar* was a good two hours late he was in good fettle by the time he met the 'Chentleman'. There is a particularly twisty bit of the road south of Knock farm, and with Baldie's judgement being more than a little affected by the drams and while he was showing off his ability as a whip, he completely misjudged a narrow bridge and 'couped' the pony and trap and the 'chentleman' in a burn! I shudder to think what The Squire had to say to Baldie, but as far as Ben Coutts is concerned the 'Baldies' are sadly all too hard to find nowadays in this age of greed and haste.

6
Rhum Ponies, Cattle and Folk

My first Highland pony—although she belonged to Glenartney I looked on her as mine way back in 1933—was bred on Rhum. She was chestnut with a silver mane and tail, so I called her 'Silver'. To this day this unusual colour can be found in the Rhum ponies.

The Rhum ponies were mentioned by Dr Johnson in his *Journey to the Hebrides*, as he was a guest of the Laird of Coll who also owned Rhum. This laird was obviously one of the better lairds, of whom all too little is heard or written about, and didn't evict his tenants as other landlords in the Highlands did. He realised however that most of the people on Rhum, which couldn't be cultivated to feed the inhabitants because of its poor and shallow soil, would be better to emigrate. It always amazes me in this so-called enlightened age that so many get hot under the collar about what are called 'The Clearances'. Of course there were some horrendous cases of poverty and hardship, and of course there was 'wailing and gnashing of teeth' when certain estates were (so-called) cleared. The Duke of Sutherland is the landlord always cited. But many who go into print or broadcast against the Clearances have never managed an acre of that land. I have in my lifetime managed tens of thousands of acres of it, and there's no way a family, expanding each year, could survive on some of that land, never mind prosper. And what a grand job most of those 'cleared' Highlanders did in what used to be known as our Colonies, Canada, Australia, New Zealand etc., not to mention south of the border and in London. Before the war it was said that if you went to see the head of a British business or bank he was bound to be a Scot!

But back to ponies and Dr Johnson's pal, Maclean of Coll. He bought a pony from one of his tenants who refused to sell it except at a high price, as the pony, and I quote, was 'of shape uncommonly elegant'. The price was one guinea and a half! Changed days.

After Maclean of Coll had the island it was sold to the Marquis of Salisbury in 1840. His son, Lord Arthur Cecil, was sure the Rhum ponies were direct descendants from Spanish horses carried on the Armada fleet that was wrecked on the Western Isles all those years before. The Lord Cecil and his brother took a whole bunch of Rhum ponies to Hatfield in 1862, and had one helluva job breaking them as they were fairly old, had seen few human beings and were stallions. The ones they did

A shooting party in front of Kinloch Castle, Rhum
(Scottish National Heritage)

break, however, showed some of the traits that we, who love and use the breed, enjoy. He talks about their staying power and their longevity. He describes them trotting for twelve miles in fifty-five minutes after they were twenty years of age, and says that they could gallop and jump. He also points out that all Rhum ponies had hazel-nut brown eyes. It's significant that the Salisbury family took them to improve the New Forest ponies, in which they had an interest, as they felt 'they had good hind quarters and their tails were well set up'. I fear that New Forest Pony breeders will not be amused to know that they had to turn to the 'Hairy Highlands' to improve those two essential points in a pony.

But we in the Highland Pony Society, as I wrote in the last chapter, have a lot for which to thank an out-cross with other breeds. Rhum, which now belongs to the Scottish Natural Heritage, was probably most famous—or infamous—in the time when Sir George Bullough owned it. He bought it from the Salisburys in 1888, and took over the island lock, stock and barrel, including the Highland Pony Stud. He paid one hundred and fifty thousand pounds for it compared with the twenty-six thousand, four hundred and fifty-five paid by the Marquis of Salisbury in 1845. Huge prices, when one thinks of the way the pound has been devalued over the years. Why I say Sir George's time was infamous was that he built Kinloch Castle in red Arran sandstone, which was completely out of keeping with the architecture of the islands.

In Archie Cameron's super book about life in Rhum written in 1988 he describes just how tough times were then for those 'Folk bred in the Highlands'. His father, though only on one pound a week pay, was determined that the family should have a Christmas present, although Christmas wasn't recognised then as it is today in Scotland. The presents were chosen from a catalogue sent from Glasgow, the usual way of buying in the West Highlands pre-war. One year the MacBrayne boat the *Plover* didn't make it, and the contents of the Christmas stockings were a mutton bone, with 'quite a bit of meat on it' Archie said, an orange which his mother said must have been dropped by Santa, as Rhum didn't grow oranges, and a scone with plenty of butter and jam on it! I wonder what the faces of modern children would look like if they got those presents in their Xmas stockings!

Sadly, according to Archie, the worst vermin in the West Highlands were midges and factors, and the latter he reckoned worse than the former. I say sadly, because for half a century I made my living as one of those he hated. However I hope I got on better with my employees and tenants than the factor on Rhum seemed to do. It was Wendy Wood, the great Scottish Nationalist, who said the three curses of the Highlands were Bracken, Braxy and MacBraynes. Braxy, although a fatal disease in sheep, always affected the fattest and fittest, but luckily their meat was perfectly edible and was a great standby for families in places like Rhum, and your author ate his share when he was shepherding in Ettrick in the thirties. Archie, like Wendy, wasn't over fond of MacBraynes, who controlled all the ferry services to all the west coast islands. If it was rough then the *Plover*, which supplied Rhum and Eigg, would miss out Rhum and dump all the passengers on Eigg. What a man Archie had for a father, as when Archie's sister, coming back from Oban High School, was unceremoniously dumped on Eigg, not Rhum, Archie's father and a pal set out in an open boat to row to Eigg, fifteen miles, in some of the wildest seas around Scotland. I don't know how many of you readers have used those old fashioned sweeps that they used then as oars—I have, and no way even in my young and fit days could I have done more than a mile or two in open sea, and they did thirty miles! They bred them tough in the Highlands then, and the tradition of educating one's family better than one was educated oneself persisted, which was why Archie's sister was sent to Oban High. The modern *Isle of Mull* steamer is full first thing on Monday morning taking children to Oban High, but the take-away food they eat is rather different to the oatmeal, braxy mutton and venison that Archie's sister would have had to supply to the landlady where she stayed during term time.

But although denigrating MacBrayne like so many of his generation, Archie was full of admiration for 'Squeaky' Robertson's captaincy of his boats and general seamanship. No wonder, when one reads that the *Plover* that did the Barra-Rhum-Eigg run was top heavy and the accommodation for passengers quite appalling. The animals being transported were in the same part of the ship as the third-class passengers, and it is said the stench of urine, dung and vomit was overwhelming after a rough crossing, of which there were and are all too many in winter time. The rounding of the dreaded Ardnamurchan point was feared then as it is to this day, for all the advances we've seen in the ships and weather forecasting. It seems in those far off days that pedigree animals, bulls, stallions etc. were specially dealt with, being swung over the side in a sling and then attached to a row boat. Ordinary animals were dumped overboard and 'the de'il tak the hindmost'. They were rounded up on landing from different beaches on the island. Archie tells a new, to me, Squeaky story about a bull being slung on board. Squeaky was not at all pleased with the way the man in charge of the derrick was lowering the bull and shouted, 'Mind his balls!' much to the embarrassment of some English passengers.

I've said before and I say again what a man Squeaky was, as were his fellow skippers on the MacBrayne fleet. They didn't need charts, they knew by heart every cluster of rocks, the currents, the tides etc. One time Squeaky had on board an Admiral in the Royal Navy who had sailed on the west coast during the First World War. He was sure that Squeaky was sailing his ship onto some rocks and demanded to see the ship's charts. These were eventually produced, covered in dust—Squeaky never used them, as he knew every inch of the waters he sailed in. The Admiral triumphantly jabbed his finger at the point on the chart where the boat was sailing and said 'I told you, Robertson, we are sailing directly into those rocks', pointing at some black dots on the chart. To which Squeaky replied 'If I didn't know these dots were fly sheet [shit] you'd be right'. Exit the Admiral.

But the man behind the whole pony set-up on Rhum in the Bullough days was Angie. Each year the ponies were brought off the hills and the surplus ones were destined for a sale in Oban. His methods of breaking ponies are not what we use today, but they seemed to succeed. He obviously had a great way with ponies, and

The 'Spanish John' landing craft, used for transporting ponies and cattle, at Rhum Pier
(Scottish National Heritage)

even when they were being shipped from pier to ferry to be slung onto the *Plover* they seemed to trust him. He must have been very strong, as he used to go into the middle of a mob of ponies, select the one he wanted and then do a 'wild west' act after grabbing it by the neck: he would twist the pony round so forcing it to the ground, then would put his thumb and forefinger in the pony's nostrils and put a halter on it. I suspect what is described as a halter was in fact a head collar, as to put a halter on a beast with one's hand on the beast's nose is impossible, unless the halter was already over Angie's arm, but I'm only quoting Archie Cameron. Then Angie would get them 'yoked' (attached), first to a log and then to harrows. After attaching the latter Angie had been seen being pulled along on his belly behind the harrows, as the pony had taken off, but he never let go the reins! Some man, but I can think of easier ways of breaking ponies, easier both to man and beast! It seems that Sir George, for all the faults Archie and others of his ilk felt the wealthy lairds had, was fond of his ponies and regularly visited the horse boxes where the breeding mares were kept. As I've said, I'm sad that Archie was 'agin' factors, but no wonder when he was sacked for 'borrowing' one of the Laird's boats and fined one pound by the factor, at a time when, as an under-gardener his weekly wage was shillings. Archie wrote to the Laird complaining about the injustice but the letter never got to the Laird. It was kept by the factor, one Bremner, who did nothing to enhance the reputation of my calling.

The problem with all too many Highland estate factors was, and sadly is, that they have never done the practical jobs that their employees do. I am eternally grateful that for all my faults as a factor, and I had many, I had been a ponyman and ghillie, I had shepherded, I had lived in a bothy (for two and a half years of my life) and so I knew a lot of my employees' problems. Even today too many young lads who are responsible for some of the finest men it has been my privilege to know, and looking after the most beautiful country in the world (and I've been able to compare it to the Americas, Africa, most of Europe, Australia, New Zealand and Denmark) have soap behind their ears: they depend too much on their computers and not enough on how the men on the ground 'tick'.

The Rhum stud will have flourished for longer than any other, albeit under many different owners. Sir George Bullough bought the best stallions he could lay his hands on, and 'Claymore', which was by 'Rory of the Hills', proved very successful, as did some of those that belonged to Lord Arthur Cecil to whom Sir George sent some of his mares. These stallions would of course be Rhum-bred, or at least have Rhum blood in their veins. Carefully line-bred stock can be terrific, whereas closely inbred stock can give you absolute rubbish, but Sir George being a racing man would know what he was about.

The Blackfaced, three-year-old wether sheep that came off Rhum, in the days when people were working physically and wanted well-hung mutton, not lamb, were famous. But with the advent of deer stalking, as it was one of the 'in' sports for the *nouveau riche*, the sheep, and shepherds, were cleared off the island and the deer stocks were allowed to increase. These were greatly improved by importing stags from some of the English 'stately homes' deer parks. I'm always sad when I hear that

'Claymore'. Not my type of Highland pony, but he won First Prize at the Highland Show and was used extensively in Rhum (John M. Macdonald)

a sheep stock is to be cleared because the owner wants to have only deer. Sad, because in my experience deer and sheep go extremely well together if the numbers are properly controlled. This is one of the real problems in the Highlands today, in that certain areas have become hopelessly overstocked with one or the other, with real damage to the environment. In some areas there are too many sheep, put there by farmers wanting more of the headage payments. In other places there is a problem because of lax shepherding, when the sheep are never moved out and in on a hill as they used to be, i.e. herded out to the tops in the morning so that they would graze their way down by the afternoon or evening. Now they are, in too many hill farms, allowed to remain in one spot completely ruining that area.

Then there are the deer forest owners who have not culled their hind stocks properly, and as a result, aided by some exceptionally mild winters, deer numbers in certain areas in the Highlands have escalated dramatically. It always amazes me that more people who love to pitch their ability of stalking against the red deer's fantastic eyesight and sense of smell don't want to stalk the hinds, which are miles more alert than some dozy old stag that is probably clapped out with guarding his harem from other stags and attending to his harem's sexual requirements. I suppose it's partly because those who pay large amounts to either own or rent a deer forest want trophies, in the shape of mounted heads or antlers, to show off their prowess. Or it may be to do with the fact that the stag-stalking season is one of the loveliest times of the year in the Highlands. As I pen this chapter in September, 1996, I am looking out to the southern slopes of the Grampians, the air is crystal clear, there isn't a cloud in the sky, the colours are out of this world and there is a slight but steady breeze from the north. Instead of concentrating on Rhum my thoughts are of days of this sort on Gaick, Ben Challum, Ardkinglas, Cluny, 'the high Tops of Blackmount', yes, and many other places I've been lucky enough to stalk.

But old age doesn't come singly, and I'm lucky to be alive and have those happy memories of halcyon days. But then some of the days hind shooting were not so halcyon, as their permitted stalking season in November, December and January could give one some stinking awful days, with snow blinding one's view and rifle sights, hurricane winds, freezing cold rain that felt like red hot needles on my all too tender skin and those half-frozen burns and rivers, all too full after melting snow, over which one had to drag the hind. So thinking back over the differences between the stag and the hind stalking I can see why the 'gentry' favour the former. But until the hind population is controlled, no way will the deer numbers be brought back to the sort of figure that the Highlands can sustain without spoiling the environment.

But back to Rhum, where in 1971 the Nature Conservancy which then owned the island decided that they had to get back to a more balanced system of grazing. To do this they wanted to start once again with cattle, which take off the top roughage of pasture, as opposed to sheep and deer which are selective feeders. So through their then Factor, Tony Hardie, I was asked to find twenty pedigree Highland heifers to establish a fold of Highland cattle. Looking back over those twenty-five years one realises (a) how much the pound has devalued and (b) how the breed is being much more properly valued.

I started by going to the February Sales in Oban, where there were but six heifers on offer that were accredited, i.e. tested free of T.B. and abortion. Of these I bought three at an average of one hundred and forty guineas. The total entry of that year was twenty-nine animals, bulls and heifers, changed days indeed when one sees what has happened since, with a resurgence of people with an acre or two wanting some nice cattle to look at, and the short-lived tremendous demand from Germany before the B.S.E. war. More recently there has been the demand for natural beef fed on the hills and uplands and given time to mature without all those dicey foods that triggered off the B.S.E. scare.

Eventually I managed to purchase the twenty heifers required to found the fold in Rhum. It is interesting to people of my age group to look back over the last quarter of a century and see the breeders who supplied me, those who had the faith, courage (and, in many cases) the sheer hard cash to keep the breed flag flying. The heifers I bought at the sale were from Ormsary, which is still going strong, owned now by Sir William Lithgow, whose father Sir James before him and whose managers and the redoubtable cattleman 'Baldie' Galbraith have been great supporters of the breed.

I got others from Scone Palace, then owned by 'Mungo', the Earl of Mansfield, but sadly sold up just before the fantastic rise in the Society's fortunes thanks to the German demand. I fear yet another wrong decision on this occasion by one of the rising number of agricultural 'consultants' who never 'consult' those of us who have been doing the practical side of the industry. Another source was Auchnacraig in Mull, at that time owned by Mrs 'Bobs' de Klee, one of this country's great ladies, whom I have mentioned in the Mull chapter. One only has to look at the present day sale catalogues to see what success her son Murray is having with the fold that she built up. Shenavallie supplied two two-year-olds, and I'm glad to say that it remains very much with the breed and must be one of the oldest folds that are registered.

Inveruglas on Loch Lomond side supplied five eighteen-month-old heifers. The late Commander Duncan was a great enthusiast for the breed, but could be very brusque. I remember him phoning me when he was President in the sixties and saying 'Ben, the Council want you to stand for the presidency again,' (I had been President in 1954) 'but I think it would be unwise, don't you?' Without giving me two minutes to think about it he said 'Thanks, I thought you wouldn't want to do it.' End of any possibility of my entry in the *Guinness Book of Records*, as Chairman of Grantown, Dalmally and Braco shows and now their Hon. Vice-Presidents— and, almost, President of the Highland Cattle Society twice. When I asked Judy Bowser, one of the bastions of the breed and still going very strong, for heifers, she wrote saying why couldn't I advise the Nature Conservancy to wait until the heifer sale in October, as she was against private sales. I then pointed out that I had only managed to purchase three at the Spring sale, and when I tried to buy hers, although I ran it up to my price of one hundred and forty guineas, it topped the sale at two hundred guineas. Because of this she sold me two at one hundred and twenty guineas. To complete our lot Tony Hardie and I went to Douneside at Tarland. Lady MacRobert, the chatelaine and very much the boss of the estate, was famous for presenting the country with three aircraft, Hurricanes, named Sir Ian, Sir Roderick and Lady MacRobert. The one in her own name was given in memory of a son killed before the war and the first two in memory of her sons killed in the defence of this country.

The cattle for Rhum were marshalled in Corson's Oban Mart but as the landing craft used by the Nature Conservancy weren't able to load the cattle in Oban it was decided to load them on a beach to the north of the town. Luckily I was on holiday so never saw the resultant fiasco, but had I been at home, having handled stock all my days, I would have been against their plan in principle. If it was the only way they could transport them then I would have had a large pen erected from which the heifers could be transferred to the barge. Suffice to say that all hell was let loose, and the heifers high-tailed it all over the place as they didn't want to be loaded. I think it was many days before they were all gathered up and finally shipped to Rhum. But all's well that ends well, and twenty five years on the Highland Fold is doing its bit in maintaining the correct grazing on Rhum and the Highland Pony Stud is prospering. One still sees the odd chestnut pony with silver mane and tail and hazel eyes and one doesn't need to ask where it was bred.

7
Ponies and Cattle on Uist and Skye

'Oh! the far islands are putting love on me, as step I wi' my cromach to the Isles'. So go the lines of a song, *The Tangle o' the Isles*, which in my youth I often sang, little realising how true they were to be for a chap called Ben Coutts. They were to come true also for my daughter, Philippa. She had been working for Save the Children Fund in South Sudan and had travelled round the world previously. Now she announced that as she was about to get some leave, could I arrange a trip to the Isles, as she was beginning to realise, like many young Scots, how little she knew about her own country.

So, with her mother, off we set: me to find out about ponies and cattle in Uist and Skye, and the younger, fitter females to walk and enjoy those magical lights one can only get on the west coast of Scotland in showery weather. We were lucky in that it was only showery and not the usual deluge, coming down stair-rods.

I hadn't been in Uist for forty years, since I judged one of the best shows of Highland cattle it's ever been my privilege to attend. On that day, even though my host and I were late, we were there earlier than those showing cattle. As Daliburgh, where the show was then held, is not in 'Wee Free' territory, I was well refreshed before I started the judging of twenty unhaltered Highland cows. Great cattle, and a great privilege, which sadly, unless the Uist crofters change their stock, no one will have again. On my recent visit I was shattered to see the Heinz 57 varieties of breeding cows. European breeds may well have their place in areas where they can be well fed, at vast expense, but they were never meant for the cold windswept high rainfall areas of the west of Scotland.

However there is one stalwart supporter of the Highland cattle breed born and bred in Uist, Ena McNeil, who with her son Angus has a very useful fold which they treat traditionally. Also they farm traditionally, but Angus rightly appreciates the tremendous advantages baled silage has for an area that has a job making hay, and he now makes a business out of contracting bale silage-making on South and North Uist and Benbecula.

It's amazing to think that way back when the Islands were owned by Clan Chiefs, in the case of North Uist the MacDonalds of Clanranald, that one MacDonald chief had eighty-eight Highland bulls and six hundred cows! Naturally he would be leasing them out to his tenants, which is what the DOAS do nowadays. Sadly, however, pandering to the lobby which follows fashion, they are leasing out bulls of breeds that may make a quick buck but do nothing to improve the breeding stock of the Islands. They should remember that it is the breeding stock, whether folk, cattle, ponies or sheep, which are the basis of Island life.

Ena was most interesting about how the corncrake population had diminished. Once again, as in the case of the bull-leasing policy, bureaucrats thought they knew better than the locals. In the old days the crofters used to harvest the oats or bere first, then lift the tatties and only after this, as their grass for hay was in old grass meadows, full of lovely weeds and herbs, that crop was taken last, by which time the corncrakes had flown the nest. But the bureaucrats living in what we in the Inverness NFU Council called 'The Edinburgh Kremlin', St Andrew's House, decided it was time these old meadows were ploughed up and re-seeded. For this they were willing to pay a subsidy of five pounds per acre, which was big, big money forty years ago. The crofters, never slow at accepting a hand-out, complied to a man. This meant the re-seeded fields came first in the summer work agenda, as they had to be cut early, and the result was the destruction of the corncrakes' nests. It's all right for the do-gooders in London, Edinburgh, Glasgow etc. saying how awful it was that the crofters were desecrating the corncrakes without a twinge of conscience. I wonder if they have tried to sleep surrounded by corncrakes calling all night. I know I slept better with German shells falling round our gun position in the Tobruk Garrison than I did in a tent in Machrie Bay, Arran, where we were surrounded with corncrakes. But now, as usual, there is another 'subsidey' (a much nicer word than subsidy) for the crofters to leave cutting the hay or silage until the corncrakes are hatched. What would those super folk, bred in the Highlands, do without the 'subsideys'!

Sadly, the Uists, which were famous when I was a lad for being horse-daft, have now hardly a horse on them. I remember they used to say that a Uist man would walk a mile to catch his pony in order to ride a mile with a message. They say that the reason that the Uist ponies were held in such high repute was that the chief of the Clan Ranald, back in the eighteenth century, had fought as a mercenary in a Spanish division and brought back some Spanish horses with him. Anyone who has been in Uist will realise the big difference between the west, with its machair land, and the east, with its hills and peat. They say that in the old days those in the West breeding ponies, and needing all their meagre amount of arable land for winter keep, put the ponies out to fend for themselves on the hills. When they wanted to break ponies to work they drove them down into the intervening bogs of peat, where the ponies sank up to their bellies and were haltered and man-handled out! Rather different to today's methods, but it must have worked. The sad thing to my mind is that, like most of Britain, Uist got rid of its ponies and turned to tractors in the early fifties. That super grey Ferguson which was ideal for crofters and small farmers has now run its course, and we saw them laying derelict everywhere. To buy a new one in 1997 is a very different kettle of fish, and as a small farmer of the past I realise that capital is a very hard thing to find to renew machinery etc. So could some crofters revert to buying four-legged horse power?

*Cattle crossing a kyle in Uist—not as wide as that between Skye and the mainland, but
nevertheless demonstrating that cattle will take the water when properly handled
(Angus A. MacDonald)*

Of course nowadays the Uists and Benbecula are joined by causeways, but it was
not always thus. The ford between Benbecula and North Uist was infamous, as
depending on the tides and the time of year it could be extremely dangerous, and all
too many were drowned there before the causeway was built. For the crossing,
ponies were tied to the tail of an older pony who would lead the way, and to this day
it amazes me that this method didn't put the lead pony's back out! Then the cattle
would be a problem until they could get one or two to lead the way. John Keay,
who organised a drove of cattle from Skye to Crieff in the early Eighties to re-enact
the old droving days, was beaten at the Kylerhea crossing from Skye to the mainland. In retrospect he reckoned that in the droving era one or two hardy old bullocks
who had swum the Kyles before were kept back to lead over the next batch. This
theory has been corroborated by someone I met in Uist who said 'There was no
problem if you got a leader'. Could be true of many walks of life!

The sad thing to my mind about the islanders forsaking their native Highland
cattle breed is that they were bred for the sort of herbage the island grows naturally.
Ena gave me an example of this, describing a situation when she had a bunch of pure
Highland bullocks with but one cross Jersey Highland bullock. They were given
typical island summer grazing of poor pasture, including some rushes, and all except

the cross beast continued to thrive—perhaps slowly, but that's what makes for tasty beef. The cross beast, however, couldn't digest the available food and landed in the deep freeze!

As for the ponies on Uist, the prize story must be that of 'Bain's horse'. I and many of my era thought that most of the Clydesdale cross Highland ponies have been non-starters, but 'Bain's horse' proved us wrong. This stallion was brought to Uist by a contractor from Ayrshire, one Bain, to help build the new schools which the Government wanted. It was back in 1872, and the 'horse' was a thick-set dark-brown Clydesdale. After carting during the day he was allowed (at a fee, no doubt) to satisfy the demands of the local crofters' mares. 'Moss Crop', who won the Gold Medal at the Dumfries Highland Show in 1903, had 'Bain's horse' in his pedigree. So did 'Isleman', that famous stallion owned by J. Munro Mackenzie of Calgary. But to my mind the best story about this obviously super horse took place when Bain had finished his contract for building the schools and was shipping the horse back from Lochmaddy. On board was the tenant of Vatersay coming back from his honeymoon. He took one look at Bain's stallion and decided to buy him. One can imagine the bargaining that took place, but eventually the horse was bought, to be off-shipped at Vatersay. When they got to that island there was no way they could launch a boat as the seas were so big, but they let the old horse go in. He was so long under water they thought him drowned, but no, he surfaced, made for the shore, headed straight for the farm where the work horses were haltered, got them so hot and bothered they broke their halters, and as one was in season he served her—what a horse! He was no youngster when he swam ashore to Vatersay, but he not only worked on the farm for many years but also travelled Ardnamurchan, Strontian and Morvern and was said to leave a lot of good stock.

Another of the things that saddened me in Uist was the number of old croft houses we saw that could have been renovated, but were being replaced by new box-type cottages which do not fit into the lovely scenery around them. I understand that whoever was in charge of planning permissions and grants for re-housing the crofters found it was cheaper to build the new box-type residence than refurbish the old. This to my mind is a pity compared to Skye which I visited next, where the white-washed farm and croft houses have been receiving grants and fit in so well to their surrounding districts. Could it be that different architects/bureaucrats advised differently on the two islands?

Skye I had visited more recently than Uist, when I judged the Kilmuir Show up in the north a few years ago. I got there only to find that being in a 'Wee Free' area it was dry, and one couldn't get the comforting 'refresh', so useful and essential to raise one's spirits for the judging of a Championship. One's judgement needs all the support it can get, as so much depends on it—how much an animal could be worth if it wins the coveted local Show Championship, quite apart from the kudos it gives the owner.

The first thing I noticed on this visit was that the wonderful smell of peat smoke which one encountered all over the Uists was missing. I understand that one hundred and twenty yards of peat have to be cut for two fires in a house, and as labour costs forty pounds per day peat doesn't come cheap any longer. All the same, nothing can beat it as a fire for gazing into of an evening. In my home it's a birchwood fire I look into, and what pleasure it gives me, but as for peat, there's something magical about the smell.

As we were travelling from Uist to Skye we were still able to go 'Over the Sea to Skye', Loch Maddy to Uig. I know that there has been a big anti-bridge campaign (of which a favourite niece of mine has been one of the leaders) but if I were farming on Skye I'd be all for the bridge—like a friend of mine who was taking stock to Dingwall Mart. He was four hours in a queue for the ferry and missed the sale. But of course the toll charge is ridiculously high and I'm sure by the time this book is in print it will have been reduced.

As ponies and cattle, both Highland of course, have kept a more tenacious hold in Skye than Uist I spent slightly more time there. As a boy I was deaved by my mentor, Murdo Nicholson of Ardrosstan, St Fillan's, himself a 'Sgitheanach', as to

Duntulm was, as I have stated many times, the main fold in Skye, and had great influence on the breed as a whole. This photo is all that remains of that famous fold, and as one can see the cattle are out on real hill country, not on good arable land, where sadly the breed is all too often seen today (Mr MacDonald, Duntulm)

how good the Duntulm cattle were. So that's where I went first. Nowadays Mr MacDonald of Duntulm has but few Highland cattle, and because of BSE got a poor price, three hundred and twenty-five pounds, for his two-year-old bullocks. This compares badly with the four hundred and eighty pounds they have to pay the DOAS for the hire of a Highland bull.

Mr MacDonald's diversification, which all small farmers and crofters are encouraged to do, is a first-class Highland museum. But he reckoned the best years of the Duntulm cattle were when Stewart of Ensay, from the mainland, took over the fold. That was when that great horse 'Failte Diamond' travelled that area. The stallion man was famous, not for his love of the ladies which I'm told was usual, but because, instead of walking his stallion, he rode a bicycle! In those days it was usual for a stallion to cover a five-mile radius as there were so many mares. Today the stallion would need a helicopter to fly from mare to mare, there are so few. How sad!

It's great to see the suffix of Dunvegan reappearing in the Highland Cattle Herd Book, as that name has continued to charm and excite all who love the Highlands and Islands. Dame Flora MacLeod was a great Scot who rightly foresaw the future tourism would have in the Highlands, and her grandson, John MacLeod, is now doing a first class job in promoting tourism. Through his manager, David MacDonald (not a MacLeod, I hear you say, but the MacDonalds also held considerable assets in the islands) they have built up a very nice fold of good cattle, grazing on the sort of herbage Highland cattle should graze—not heavily fertilised arable pasture, which sadly today all too many folds are on. By all means the bullocks should be grazed on good grass to finish them, but not the cows. One of the sad things at Dunvegan that David showed me was a delightfully lush area which had been famous a century ago for finishing three- and four-year-old bullocks which had commanded the top prices for any Skye Highland bullocks. Then some silly ass of a Factor (what, again?) had advised Dame Flora to plant it with my chief Highland hate, sitka spruce, and by so doing sterilised the grazing above. But bygones are bygones, and John MacLeod has gone on to do wonderful things for tourism. Quite apart from the Castle, with all its lashings of Highland sentiment, he has provided a first-class restaurant in the midst of what to me has been a gastronomic desert for years, and I'm not just thinking of Skye, I'm thinking of the Highlands as a whole. His Highland boutique, called the St Kilda Collection, so impressed my wife and daughter that my visit to Dunvegan cost me much more than I had budgeted for!

John MacLeod was more than interesting about the family history. It seems that his great-great-grandfather, during the ghastly potato famine in the mid-eighteen-forties, which devastated the West Highlands and Ireland, spent every penny he had to help his staff and his tenants (so much for the wicked landlords we are always hearing about on the media). As a result he bankrupted himself and lost the estate. This meant that a later laird had to take a job as a very poorly-paid civil servant in London. He had to travel each day on a train from Maidstone in Kent (which some poor so-and-sos are still doing) up to his work in London. I'm told that one goes into the same carriage each day and covers one's face with the *Telegraph* or the *Times*

Dunvegan Castle, Isle of Skye (John MacLeod of MacLeod)

or *Express* (I doubt if the *Independent* or the *Sun* were then born). Anyway this Chief of the Clan, who like them all would have personality and charm, sat each morning beside a fellow traveller who liked him so much he asked him to go out and look after a business in the Americas called 'Coral'—which you and I now know as Shell (hence the Coral sign on Shell petrol pumps). This MacLeod came back with enough money to buy what remained of the old Dunvegan Estate. Certain parts of the Estate, like Glenelg and St Kilda, had been sold off and it was not possible to re-unite them with the main Estate, but the majority had been retained.

Dunvegan was one of the places in Skye where cattle were bought by dealers from the mainland. It was the typical old-fashioned mart with but little of what we expect in our marts today, just cattle in bunches held there by their owners and relatives with their sticks, and all too often their unruly dogs. After the Sale the mainland dealers wanted to have their stock driven to Portree, a distance of twenty-two miles, but as they were offering one pound for the job, which was a fortune then, they had dozens of laddies willing to take it on. I met one of those laddies, Alec Nicholson from Amer. He said it was no sinecure, as some of the cattle were always turning back, and as he had to walk twenty-two miles from Dunvegan to Portree with the cattle, with two hundred in the drove, and then he had to walk nine miles home to Amer, he reckoned he had earned his one pound, and so do I!

Alec also did his stint as stallion man and travelled stallions at the age of nineteen. One which he remembers with affection was 'Knocknagael Monarch'. He always reckoned that the Uist ponies were older than the owners said: they blamed the sand in the machair on which the ponies grazed for the fact that their teeth were shorter than they should have been!

Sadly the Uists and Skye have lost one of their last great supporters of the Highland ponies in the passing of Ian Campbell of Glenelg. He, and his father Colin before him, did so much to keep the Highland pony flag flying during the post-war years when so many in the Highlands and Islands wanted to become mechanised. Sadly the Lord didn't give them the skills to deal with mechanisation that he gave them to deal with stock. It was in 1949 at Kilmuir Show that Colin Campbell judged the Highland ponies, and so liked a Duntulm mare that he bid one hundred pounds for her, a huge price back in those days, but Colin knew his ponies and he was so right as she turned out to be a super breeder. She founded a lot of his winning stock, one of which was shown by his son Ian (who died in 1996 far too early) at the centenary Black Isle Show, where I made her Champion Highland Pony.

The Black Isle, to my mind one of the best, if not the best, district shows in the country, has an overall horse championship. In the year in question that lovely lady the Queen Mother was to present the prizes. In the horse section there was this good Highland pony mare. A Welsh pony had won the Mountain and Moorland section, but the judge of that section, Peggy Grayson, a well known judge and correspondent to the *Horse and Hound,* admitted to me that although it was a good beast it wasn't as good as the Highland, and hadn't behaved as well when paraded as she would have liked, and this could cause problems if it was made overall Champion. I was adamant that Ian's mare was the best and she agreed. Then came in the judge of the thoroughbred section and started telling us (Peggy and me, as the Shetland pony judge had conceded defeat and gone home) what a marvellous specimen she had as thoroughbred champion, how it would have won at the Royal Show had it been there etc. etc. To which I replied, 'Things must have changed overnight, as I've been at the Royal almost every year since 1951 and that pony wouldn't be in the first five in its class because of etc. etc.' (naming several faults, some real, some just to make her look at her horse again). After she recovered from the initial shock she exclaimed, 'But your Highland hasn't been ridden!'—whereupon Peggy said 'I'd ride that any day, judging by the way it walks', and Ian, who was showing the mare, added, 'I'll just get a saddle and you can ride her'. But as time was running out and the Champion had to be in the main ring to receive the award, I said, 'Sorry Ma'am, we are agreed that the Highland pony mare is overall horse section champion'. I thought the poor lady was going to burst a gasket, or at least a bit of her underwear, as she went into a tirade about how wrong and wicked Peggy and I had been, and then she said she'd call in an umpire, to which my response was, 'Why? It's two to one'.

So Ian's lovely mare went to receive the Championship sash from the most loved and respected Lady in the land, who has graced more Agricultural Shows than most and certainly more than any other Royal. Among the many gifts given to this gracious lady is that most important one of being able to talk, with real interest and knowledge, to any class of person. Ian Campbell phoned me up the next night and thanked me for giving him the chance of meeting and speaking to the Queen Mum. He also asked me what he should do with his good mare and my reply was immediate. 'Don't sell her, breed from her, one only breeds one or two good ones in a lifetime.'

I gave this same advice to Alastair Johnson in Uist when he asked me to value a good Highland cattle heifer he had. I'm convinced that as the number of people eating beef is going to decrease so those that continue to eat it will demand quality. What better basis for this than a good Highland heifer crossed with a Shorthorn and then mated to an Aberdeen Angus bull? To supply this, pure Highland folds will be needed.

But to return to the ponies that came from Skye, another notable mare was 'Staffin Princess', bought by my old friend Jack Cameron of Glenfinlas, as I've already said, the best showman of a Highland pony in my day. She was highly thought of by one and all, and judging by the photos of her had a super body and was right on her legs, though to my way of thinking was a bit 'long in the face': I would have liked a more pony head. But who am I to argue with Jack Cameron's judgement? He was one of my great pin-ups in my stock learning days, and a very highly respected member of the Scottish Land Court.

And of course in a book of this sort one must relate how the Highland ponies of Skye in the old days (which I wish we still lived in) were used in wagonettes to take the lairds or big farmers to market days, or used as saddle ponies for those of lesser means to move around. These days one can hardly drive safely any more, as all drivers seem to want to emulate Jim Clark or Jackie Stewart on those tortuous one-track roads. Back in the late eighties the tenant of Duntulm used a pair of smashing-looking black Highland ponies which were very fast, they were father and son although the father had been gelded late in life. Duntulm was always driven by his coachman to Portree market (long gone) where he enjoyed dramming in the company of his neighbour Kingsburgh. He hailed from England and had brought a pair of fast trotting ponies from the south with him. They challenged each other to match their respective pairs driven by their coachmen, with the respective owners ensconced in the back, over a two-mile course on the Portree-Uig road. They tossed for 'pole position' and Kingsburgh won. Given the narrowness of the roads in Skye (they were even narrower then) he must have thought he was home and dry. They both set off at a great pace, but after a mile Duntulm's pair were literally breathing down Kingsburgh's neck. Being the gentleman he was he told his coachman to pull in and let Duntulm past. At the end of the two miles they both dismounted, shook each other's hands, then Duntulm took out his flask and they drank to the two black Highland ponies. How civilised they were in those days!

One of those two black ponies was grandsire to the famous 'Rory o' the Hills' which I wrote about in the Mull chapter. What I didn't know about him until I went to Skye was that, like 'Bain's horse', Rory was being shipped to the mainland, probably to go down a coal mine, when he was spotted by the Laird of Strathaird who bought him. He used him, then the horse went to Castles Estate, Lochawe, and so to 'the Squire' at Tiroran. Rory had started life at Talisker, then owned by a Mr Ferguson and now run as a first class Bed & Breakfast residence.

Another horse bred on Skye was 'Allan Kingsburgh', which was purchased by the Lord Lovat of his day. This horse not only made his name by leaving a lot of good stock in the Airds district of the Lovat Estates, but was also known as a great swimmer. It seems that Allan was sent to Glendoe, on the south side of Loch Ness and near Fort Augustus, didn't like it, swam the Loch, which is a mile across at that point, and arrived back at Beaufort, a distance of some miles, the next morning—some horse! I was more than interested in this story because in the fifties George Mackie (now Lord George Mackie CBE, DSO, DFC, LLD) and I did an advisory job for the then owner.

So without a doubt Uist and Skye had a tremendous effect on the foundation stock of both Highland ponies and cattle. Although because of changing circumstances there is no way either breed will have such a part to play in those islands' economy again, there are still a few Folk left who can remember 'the days that once were'.

8

The Royals' Interest in All Things Highland: People, Land, Ponies and Cattle

It always annoys me when some of the SNP say they want to do away with the Royal Family. I often wonder if they have ever considered how much the Royals have done for Scotland, and especially the Highlands, in this last century.

It was back in 1847 that Queen Victoria rented Ardverikie Estate, on which I was to be a tenant from 1951-59. Ardverikie is on Loch Laggan, and anyone who knows the weather in the Highlands knows that the way the wind is blowing (usually from the south-west) dictates what sort of weather one is to get. Luckily for Deeside it never stopped raining when Queen Victoria was at Ardverikie. I say lucky, because at the time Queen Victoria's doctor's son was in Deeside, at Tillypronie. His advice was, 'Why not get Her Majesty to come over here, as we've had unbroken sunshine!'

The rest is history. Having had the honour of going to Balmoral for different reasons I know by the number of cars in the car park and the jams on the roads on the Braemar Games day just how much Royalty have helped that Highland area. Speaking as a hill farmer I know it would not be possible to make the sort of living we all expect nowadays without other sources of income, and that has to come from the tourists that the Royal connection has brought into the area.

I personally will never forget the Ardverikie area, not only because I love the challenge which the high hill areas of Scotland present to a farmer, but also because of the fact that my first family look on Gaskbeg at Lagganbridge as home.

It is also memorable to me for one of those bizarre occasions that only happen occasionally, but that stay with one always. That area of Ardverikie was between the Protestant and Catholic divide, the Protestants I think got defeated by the terrain and the climate! There was a lovely wee Roman Catholic church and cemetery between Lagganbridge and Loch Laggan in which a well-respected Laird from the Spean Bridge area was to be interred. As it was midsummer and I was up to my eyes in sheep work I said I couldn't go to the house but would be at the graveyard. The burial service was to be performed by the Laird's brother. The Laird, like many Highland lairds, had been a regular soldier to keep his wee estate going (and it was either the Forces or the Church for those families as the estates couldn't keep them at home.) Imagine the scene, one of those hot sticky August days, the coffin being borne along by estate employees, with reinforcements, at least a five-mile journey,

Queen Victoria, a great devotee of Highland ponies, riding up the slopes of Lochnagar.
She must have been a tough cookie judging by some of the rides she undertook
(The Royal Collection © Her Majesty the Queen)

and everyone on the way plying them with a 'refresh'. We at the cemetery had been
waiting well over half an hour beyond the allotted time with the midges biting one
and all—and especially under my kilt!—when a very unsteady lot of pallbearers hove
into sight! When they got to the bottom of the wee brae that led up to the cemetery
they were all about to sit down. I will never forget the purple-clad priest, who had
been pacing up and down for half an hour, shouting at the pallbearers: 'Come on
with the bloody Colonel, boys!'—and they very unsteadily did!

Queen Victoria must have been really hardy, as she rode the famous ride from
Linn o' Dee to Blair Atholl via Glen Tilt in October. In those days, of course, she
rode side-saddle. Sally, my wife, did the same ride a couple of years ago riding
astride, and told me there were sheep paths which, when one looked down from
them, were quite frightening, and she certainly wouldn't have done it side-saddle!
There are many pictures of Queen Victoria riding Highland ponies, always of course
with a vast retinue of pipers, ghillies, etc. This is rather different from our modern
Royals, who rightly try, when in the Highlands, to enjoy the hills and the sport they
provide with as few staff as is necessary; the decent souls have to put up with enough
security and media attention when they are in the south. But by what one has read
of Queen Victoria's son 'Teddy' I don't think he enjoyed the hair-shirt existence
that Balmoral would demand in the last century, and so he wouldn't come in contact
with Highland ponies much—though Munro MacKenzie sold 'Skerryvore' to Balmoral during Teddy's reign.

Great fame, however, was brought to the breed when King George V's equerry,
Sir Arthur Erskine, bought 'Jock' from a Major Logan of Inverness. 'Jock' was by
the great 'Glenbruar', and many who saw him said he should never have been castrated;

but perhaps, like many things in life, 'it's an ill wind…' Jock literally followed his master to his grave, as he walked after King George's coffin. Although there was no TV in those days a film was made, and those who frequented the 'flickers', as we called them, would see this handsome animal, many if not most seeing a Highland pony for the first time. Those who saw that film say he was a wonderful specimen of the breed with his flowing mane and tail, and always beautifully presented by his groom. The thing that I admired about this pony, going by the records, is that King George liked him because 'he was not too fast or too slow, had a perfect mouth and a comfortable trot.' What more could an old man want in a horse? So no wonder King George had Jock sent to Sandringham, where he took him to his pheasant shoots, and then back up to Balmoral for the 'Glorious Twelfth' (and the twelfth *was* 'glorious' in the twenties and thirties, when grouse moors were properly burnt, keepered and not over-grazed.)

I have no record of George VI's involvement with the breed, but our present Monarch is a tremendous supporter and patron of both the Highland pony and Highland cattle breeds. She has done extremely well in the show ring with the former and both the show and sale ring with the latter. Her Majesty is always most generous in her praise of the work put into both breeds by her Factor, Martin Leslie. I often wish more employers were less stingy in their praise of those who have organised the breeding of the stock that has won them championships and has made them big prices. They could be much more appreciative of their ponymen and

King George V with his faithful 'Jock', who literally followed him to his grave
(John M. Macdonald)

cattlemen (or women, of whom there are many today who are absolutely 'the tops'). Having said that, I am not thinking of any of my former employers, but rather of the people who have made money in other businesses and take a liking to Highland ponies or cattle. They employ someone who knows about the job, they win trophies or make a big price, and then forget about the person who did the hard graft! Oh yes, in my fifty years in the stock business I've seen it all too often.

One of the things I like about the Balmoral Stud is that all the ponies have to work. When Her Majesty graciously granted me an audience to discuss her stud we were talking about the advisability or otherwise of taking mares to the hill with foal at foot. I've always liked the idea, as they learn about crossing burns properly, not jumping them as I've seen too often with deer saddle slipping or panniers flapping. Her Majesty agreed, but said the foals could get very spoilt—perhaps the Royal lunches are more tasty than our bothy-made 'pieces'!

We agreed about the tremendous difference in development of the Highland pony over the years. Her Majesty said that the first she rode was so sprung in the rib and bad shouldered that when she dismounted our future Queen felt she might be bandy-legged for life! Perish the thought and thank God it never happened! How wise ponies can be compared with horses was a subject on which we both agreed. Her Majesty had been at the head of the file going out for a day's stalking one day, riding a Highland pony. All of a sudden he came to a dead stop, and nothing Her Majesty, a highly accomplished horsewoman, could do would move him. Then the head stalker came past to 'spy' the corrie. When he waved back, on moved the pony as he'd been trained to do. I told the story of old Tam Dow having had one over the eight and being taken home by his Dunira-bred pony up Glenlednock. The river was in spate, and no way could Tam get the pony to cross, but when he woke shivering in the morning he realised that pony had saved his life.

At Balmoral there are twelve ponies used for trekking in June, July and early August and then they go to work on the hill, either with panniers for the grouse or deer saddles for the stalking, or both. Of these there are five Highlands, as well another two which pull a cart-load of visitors around the grounds. The rest are Fells, and as Her Majesty said, 'I suppose we were just given them sometime'! But my goodness, hasn't the Duke of Edinburgh done well driving the Balmoral team of Fells?

For too long certain breeders have bred ponies and done nothing with them except show them in hand at the summer shows, and all too often they are so fat that they can't move. But even the stallions at Balmoral are broken to ride and 'Balmoral Dee' and 'Balmoral Chieftain' have both won their ridden classes at the Highland Show. When 'Balmoral Chieftain' won, 'Balmoral Moss' was in the same class and was well down the line. Chieftain had been sold, as he was no good at coming down a steep hill with a stag aboard, and Moss had been retained, and is now the stud horse in Aberdeenshire. I was amused however that Her Majesty, like any ordinary person who shows ponies, or any stock for that matter, was not pleased that a pony of her breeding should beat a pony that she had retained. But then one tends to forget that

Our monarch, a great supporter of the breed, with the Duke of Edinburgh in front of Balmoral, surrounded by their Highland ponies (P.J. Ord, Balmoral Estates Office)

the Royals are human as are we ordinary mortals, and sadly some of the young ones have all too many of the failings that ordinary folk have.

When talking about ponies, stalking and hill management in general Her Majesty showed the same sense of humour that I had encountered so often when talking to her mother, and when we were agreeing how sad it was that so many townees were devoid of any knowledge of country matters she told a story. It seems when one of her ponymen was coming off the hill leading his pony, complete with a stag on board, a bus load of old ladies were just disembarking. One old lady looked terribly shocked, and said, 'What did the poor beast die of?' Quick as a flash came the reply, 'Lead poisoning, Lady'—a reply which the Queen and I thought not only quick thinking but very funny.

As for the Highland cattle fold at Balmoral, it was only founded in 1954 and has had great success in show and sale ring. Until the Pennygowan Bull made twenty thousand guineas in 1992 the Queen had the top-priced Highland Bull on two occasions and the championships at their respective Bull Sales in Oban, not bad going by any standards.

The chieftain of my Clan (the Coutts being a sept of the Farquharson), one Captain Alwyn Farquharson, won his first Championship at Oban in October 1995 after XYZ years of trying, although he owned two folds, one in Deeside at Invercauld and one in Mull at Torloisk. Both were old-established folds, the latter originally belonging to his uncle, Major Compton. I'm told the Major owned all the docks area at Portsmouth, quite a handy source of revenue to bolster up a Highland estate. Having managed a few in the last half century, believe me when I say they need a hefty input from some other source. This is another subject on which the Monarch and I agreed, about this silly notion some have that Highland estates should be viable. There is no way with our modern standard of living this can be made to work, and unless the hill areas are subsidised we will see the greatest clearances since the infamous ones all those years ago.

I was lucky to see a lot of the Royal Fold, as the Highland Cattle Society asked me to be presenter on a video that they were making about the breed. Obviously the Royal Fold was a *must* to be included, not only because it would help sell the video, especially overseas, but because the Fold are managed as Highland cattle should be managed. They are outwintered, in their case in birch woods and in a hard cold environment, the cows not pushed or overfed. Then only the best bull calves are kept entire and the best of the heifers retained for stock, with the others being sold off. In the 1995 October Sales the Queen's third prize heifer made two thousand five hundred guineas in a sale where there were no overseas buyers because of the stupid BSE scare. So I was more than proud to be allowed to see the Fold for a day or two, in fact it was more or less a private viewing.

Andrew Laing, a breed Society President some years after me, laid the foundations of the Royal Fold, and a typically sound job he made of it. Andrew had started his training for his life as an Estate Factor in the Dalmally office of the Breadalbane Estate, which in those far-off days was responsible for tenant farmers who owned Highland cattle folds. It was still true then, as in the words of the poem:

'From Kenmore (Loch Tay) to Ben More (Mull) the land is a' the Marquis's...'

The Marquis mentioned is the Marquis of Breadalbane, second only to the Chief of the Campbell clan. The chieftain was the Duke of Argyll and resident in Inveraray Castle; he owned, in the days of that poem, the whole of Kintyre.

When Andrew was under-factor in Dalmally the Breadalbane fortunes were fading fast. They were not helped by ostentatious visits by the Duke to the Earl of Richmond and Gordon at Goodwood, complete with pipers, ghillies etc. all decked out in full Highland regalia, and his love of gambling. This all had to be paid for by rents from land that I call 'miles and miles of damned all'! So Andrew's early experience would not have been easy. He told me he was always being told to jack up the rents, which after the collapse of the sheep trade in 1922 was impossible. The tenants, with whom he got along very well, were always wanting more done. Andrew was finding after the first war, as I did after the second one, that farmers and crofters who had been away from home, seeing cities overseas and experiencing other ways of life, when they came home weren't willing to put up with things like the 'Thunder Box' at the bottom of the garden. In my case they wanted electricity, and I suppose now the modern factor will need to see that there is a double garage to house the posh four-wheel drive vehicle as well as the clapped-out old Subaru the farmer drives. But Andrew survived his time in Dalmally and 'got an eye for a beast', as we say in the stock world when someone knows what makes a good animal. I'm sad he didn't live to see the terrific entries (over one hundred) that are shown at Dalmally in the Highland Cattle classes in the nineties, and I'm proud to say that I was the one who started them when I was the Show Chairman in 1960.

Andrew went on to form his own factor's business called Laing and Lyle in the county of Angus, and not only bought the foundation stock for Balmoral but also bought and managed the Findrack Fold for Colonel Crabbe. Andrew was highly respected, although some of the cattlemen said he was 'more an actor than a factor', solely because he always, even when judging cattle, wore a hard Trilby hat turned up at the brim, and a suit, as opposed to the deerstalker and plus-fours which was the more usual dress for factors judging stock in those days. But whoever advised the Royals to use Andrew had the right idea, as he was knowledgeable and honest. He went to factor the Pollock Estate in Glasgow, and look at the success that fold of cattle have had.

Estate factors (agents in England) have always been an integral part of the estate structure in the Highlands, and Balmoral is no exception. I didn't know many of Martin Leslie's predecessors, but Martin would be one of the few Scottish factors who had bred and trained gun dogs so well that when he retired from being factor at Balmoral his German pointers were in demand the length and breadth of Scotland. My first acquaintance with him was when, like me, he had failed his veterinary exams, he in the fifties, I in the thirties, and he came to pick up grouse at Glentromie, an estate I was managing in Badenoch, with a really well-trained black Labrador. It was, by the way, at my appointment as factor of Glentromie and Gaick that I learnt what the average keeper/stalker thinks of estate factors when I approached the head stalker, rather timidly as I was only in my thirties, and enquired, 'Any problems with vermin here?' Back came the reply, 'Only a puckle hoodie crows and a factor'!

You may think I have dwelt too long on the subject of factors in a chapter concerning the Royal involvement with Highland ponies and cattle. My reason for doing it is that the Royals, like many Highland landlords, are dependent on their factors if they are to be able to have a trouble-free holiday on their estate. Believe me, there can be all too many problems, and I can speak as one who has factored ten different estates in the last fifty years. The worst problems arise from personality clashes where a few families are having to live side by side all the year round. Often the men can get along together because of their common interest in their jobs, but oh boy! look out if the wives start rowing. If I had to build workers' cottages for a laird on an estate I'd have them built as far apart as possible, so that the wives didn't squabble over whose kids were misbehaving or whose washing on the line was a disgrace and it was time that she bought her husband some new combinations. Sounds ridiculous, but I've had that complaint! Then, next to the people, one of the worst problems is dry rot, the curse of most old shooting lodges and castles. In the West Highlands with its high rainfall, roofs, and especially lead gutterings which become perforated with age, can be a real headache. And of course the owners and their factors do not always see eye to eye on how an estate should be managed. Balmoral has at the time of writing, April 1996, a new factor. I wish him well, and may there be continued success for the Royal stud of ponies and fold of Highland cattle.

Postscript. Sadly, since I penned the above, the Royal stud has had at least one case of the dreaded grass sickness. As this disease, which has raged for half a century and more without any cure being found, is especially prevalent in young stock, Her Majesty's home-bred young stock are being kept in one of her southern studs, and older ponies are being hired to do the work at Balmoral. It would seem that this dreaded disease has no concessions to make even to Royalty!

9
Highland Cattle

I suppose childhood memories are always very special, as one never remembers any of the bad times, only the good ones. At St Fillan's, where we holidayed, I can't remember any wet days, and there must have been many, but only those wonderful picnics we had, having rowed our ancient boat a good three and a half miles up the Loch, on what always seemed in retrospect to be wonderfully sunny days, when I'll bet half the time it was coming down stair-rods!

But one memory that I will take to my grave with me is of the day when old Murdo Nicholson, the local farmer, for whom I milked his kicking heifers, repaid me by taking me to Oban to see my first Highland cattle sale. For the life of me I can't remember the year, but it would be about 1929 as we were in Arran in 1930. The rail journey from St Fillans to Balquhidder junction was pure magic, as was the one from Balquhidder through Glenogle and on to Crianlarich, and whoever allowed Beeching to scrap it should have had his head looked at!

When we got to Oban Murdo was surrounded by friends, as he was a 'Sgitheanach', born in Skye, and the Oban autumn sales were used by all islanders as a meeting place for gossip and a spree! I will always remember Murdo saying, 'There's nothing to beat the "Duntulm" cattle,' (being from Skye, of course) and although I knew little about the finer points in those far-off days I suppose I had 'an eye for a beast', as I could see they were well shaped compared with many others. As the day wore on Murdo became more and more talkative, as he kept going off for a 'refresh' with his pals. As he was an elder in the church, and knowing father was a Church of Scotland minister, he kept saying 'I've chust had another lemonade, Ben.' But even then I knew he wasn't smelling of lemonade! In those days the cattle came off the boats and were herded through the town, and on these occasions I've seen Highland bullocks cause havoc in a vegetable shop. No wonder, if they came off one of the islands and suddenly saw a juicy cabbage or some enticing carrots instead of the molinia and nardus they were used to. These are the worst and most unappetising grasses grown in the Highlands, but Highland cattle will eat them, and improve the pasture for those picky feeders, sheep.

Prince Philip recently made a crack about some folk in the West enjoying a 'wee dram' or two, and had he seen those drovers sixty years ago it would have proved his point. The October Sales were the culmination of their year, they were tipped by those selling and those buying cattle, and they were facing six months of unemployment, an all too usual prospect in those days, so they got gently fu', but the cattle always got to the mart. I often wonder when I go to Oban in the Nineties, as I do at least three times a year, what the modern shopkeepers would think of cattle literally taking over the town. Then Oban was an agricultural town, but now, sadly for us oldies, it has been taken over by the tourists, and take-away restaurants and cheap 'gee-gaw' shops are the order of the day. No longer would the shopkeepers tolerate a Highland bullock leaving his trade mark at the shop's front door!

When the cattle were sold they went south by railway, either the LMS (London, Midland and Scottish) or LNER (London North Eastern Railway) which had wonderfully-built wooden cattle trucks for commercial cattle and padded trucks for horses or pedigree bulls. I well remember Robert Mair, who was much respected as Thomas Corson's chief auctioneer (having said that, he was only promoted from being chief clerk during the war, as he wasn't fit to join the forces) and highly regarded for his honesty. He was selling Highland bulls, and in came an islander who had obviously had one or two. Robert asked, 'Is he of a good strain?' Back came the reply: 'He never saw a goods train in his life, he was off the Mull boat this morning'!

As I went south to Sussex to find a job from 1936-39 and then served in the forces until 1944, it was not until that year that I came in contact with the breed again. That was the year I was fortunate enough to be appointed manager on one of Sir James Denby Roberts' farms on Strathallan Estate. The farm was Lawhill, and the tenant, one Peter Wilson, had died. His son didn't want the tenancy and so the farm reverted to the Laird, Sir James, who appointed me as manager, one of the luckiest things that has happened to me in a lucky life.

Peter Wilson had made a lot of money in dealing in cattle, especially by buying them from the islands or in Oban and taking them back to Lawhill and Mill of Gask, the best grazing farms it has been my privilege to manage. When I took over it was the November term (28th) and Peter had bought a lot of three-year-old Highland bullocks at the October Oban Sales. I was, after all, very green to the job, and had to rely heavily on Georgie Wilkie, my grieve, for advice on the arable side and Findlay Bruce, my cattleman, about stock. Gosh! what knowledge those men had, and what hours of labour they put in for but small monetary return.

Part of Findlay's perks was to graze the 'long meadow', i.e. the road, with his cow, and as the roadside verges had never seen fertiliser and were full of weeds, herbs etc., his cow's milk was sought after, locally, for butter-making. So it was to Findlay I turned when the valuation of the farm was completed and said, 'What do we do with the Highland bullocks?' 'Get the horns off them boss and put them in the reed [cattle court] for the winter and they'll thrive like mushrooms.' I'm afraid the RSPCA and the animal rights do-gooders wouldn't have approved of our methods of de-horning in those days, as we used huge big secateurs like miniature guillotines. I know it sounds cruel and they bled for a bit, but I never saw a bullock up or down afterwards and they were always ready for their next feed! I know what strong feelings there are in the country today about cruelty to animals, but I know animals don't feel pain as we do, as I have castrated thousands, yes thousands, of lambs on the hill estates I've managed. I have had only one death, and that was my fault, the rest have run off shouting for their mothers. Just try the same operation on humans and see the difference!

During my three happy years with Sir James Roberts I bought a lot of toppers of cross-Highland bullocks to finish on the lush fields of those two farms, and of course Oban was one of the main centres where one could procure them. Cross-Highland cattle are by a Beef Shorthorn bull and out of a Highland cow, and in the days when the Department of Agriculture hired good Shorthorn bulls to the islanders there were no better cattle came off the Islands. In my opinion no better cattle are coming off the Islands today, because although the Continental sires that are being used, i.e. the Charolais, Simmental and Limousin, give the islanders more profit by leaving bigger calves, their females that are retained for breeding don't like the climate and have to be discarded at a very young age.

As Sir James had a fold of Highland cattle and a Shorthorn herd, both chosen for him by that great stocksman Duncan Stewart, and because he was a Director of the Royal Show of England and through that a friend of Lord Trent's, chairman of Boots the Chemists, the latter asked him to arrange a demonstration in the Oban Mart extolling the merits of the cross-Highland bullock for beef and the heifer as breeding stock. The reason for this was that at that time there was a lot of crossing of Highland cows with Ayrshire bulls and vice versa, neither of them a good cross. Sir

Cattle on the last ever drove from Skye to Crieff, undertaken by John Keay in 1985. They are passing through Comrie, five miles from their journey's end (J. Mitchell)

James chucked the whole thing at me, saying, 'Boots Pure Drug Company are paying, so money's no object, Ben.'

Two things stand out in the memory of that demonstration, which was staged in the old Oban Mart to a packed audience. The first was the three-year-old cross-Highland bullocks, which were toppers that I'd bought in Stirling. They had to be kept at Saulmore outside Oban, on the seashore overnight, and when we went to collect them on the day of the demonstration one decided to take to the sea. It was last seen swimming in the direction of Mull (that must have put the odd halfpenny or two on Boot's drugs.) Then after it was all over I, because of shortage of petrol, was going back by bus to spend the night at Taynuilt with my friend Tommy Macdonald. I (conceitedly) had thought it had gone well. On the bus was Tommy's highly respected manager Sam MacLennan, and I said to him, bursting with pride at what I thought I had done, 'What did you think of that, Sam?' 'Well, it wouldn't do any harm,' he replied. Exit deflated Coutts.

Then there were the heady days when I worked for Duncan Stewart, one of the greatest stocksmen that Scotland has produced in my time, but sadly so shy that he let others, not half so able, but with more bullshit and less brains, trample all over him. As I know from my army days, 'Bullshit Baffles Brains', and Duncan had none of the former and lots of the latter. He it was, who, with his experience on the Shorthorn Council, got a hold of the Highland Cattle Society by the scruff of the neck, made it a new constitution, saw that Presidents didn't overstay their welcome, but if they were any good made sure they could be used as Junior Vice-President, Senior Vice-President and Past President on top of their Presidential year, made members pay realistic sums for entering cattle in the herd book, and, as it was just after the war, started a grading-up register for cattle that people knew were pedigree but hadn't been registered. But most of all he, with his vast knowledge of breeding Shorthorn cattle, set about putting flesh onto Highland cattle. These had become a breed with which, if you hadn't hair and horn, you couldn't do any good at the Highland Show, which was then everyone's ambition. At that time Islay House, owned by Major Morrison, but whose fold was run by George Bruce and John Carmichael, Auchnacloich, owned by Ernest Nelson but ruled by Duncan McNab, and Mingary, owned by Lord Trent but managed by John McCallum, ruled the roost.

Duncan Stewart's forebears came from Loch Tayside and were themselves breeders of Highland cattle, which he told me have always carried flesh, if given time. He set about improving the breed to his way of thinking. He started with a bull called 'Fearacher of Gartlea', which had a real backside on him, and also a white tip to his tail, which Duncan reckoned was a touch of Shorthorn blood, hence the backside! Then he went to Major Fletcher's at Laudale and bought every heifer he could, although he knew they were not registered or completely pure but were super cattle, good headed, right on their legs, short-backed and deep-ribbed. I can't think why modern cattle breeders turn to hill breeds like Highland ponies and cattle, Galloway cattle or Blackface sheep, and then say they don't want them with deep ribs and a 'belly', because they were bred to use the roughage of our Scottish hills, molinia, nardus and heather, not fancy made-up feeds sold at a vast price by the feed merchants today. To use that natural feed the beast must have room for roughage. One of Duncan's greatest sayings to me back in 1948 was, 'Ben, I fear the art of the feeder has taken over from the art of the breeder.' My good friend and mentor of all those forty-eight years ago, I wonder what you would think of some of the bulls that waddle round the ring at the Bull Sales today, hopelessly overfed because some scientists, who have never made or lost one penny in breeding stock, have decreed that animals should put on a certain amount of weight at a certain age. Put some of their 'super models' on the sort of grazing that their breed should have, and one realises what bunkum they talk! I suppose like us all they need a job, only I wish they would try breeding and owning some stock, and learn the hard way as some of us have had to do!

It was in 1947, the year of the great snowstorm, that Sir James Roberts kindly said to Duncan Stewart, partner in their hill estate Ben Challum Ltd, that he thought I was wasted on an arable farm and that I should be appointed manager of their hill estate. Duncan felt that as that wasn't a full time job (with only eight thousand ewes, one hundred hill cows and sixteen employees), that I should manage Millhills Estate with its one thousand acres and thirty employees, and Brae of Fordie and Balmuick with their Highland cattle folds (with one thousand sheep and four men) all for six pounds per week, plus free house, milk, meal and tatties, and free use of transport, the latter an unheard-of luxury all those years ago!

Brae of Fordie and Balmuick, the hill farms at Comrie, drew me like a magnet with their Highland cattle folds. The cattleman there was Jock Gordon, who had been with the Shorthorns at Millhills, but through no fault of his own had to be sent up to Fordie to take charge of the Highland bulls. I learnt so much from Jock, who once told me, 'Don't bother about the useless ones, make a job of the guid yins.' And how right he was. Down at Millhills there was a cattleman who brought out a whole lot of what father would call 'five-eighters'—i.e. just over half good enough, five points out of eight—but Jock and his student Sandy Gray at Millhills put all they had into one good one which paid for the rest. I remember following Jock along a passage of bull boxes. He had a bundle of hay under his oxter, and when he got to his pin-up bull he was pulling out handfuls of the sweetest smelling hay (it was lovely meadow hay in those days, full of herbs), and after he'd done that he threw the rest into the bull next door, saying, 'That'll do you, you b——, because you won't pay for your keep!'

Duncan used to name his bulls alphabetically, to go with the ear-tattooing he had introduced to the breed after the war. Say his tag was DMS (as mine was JBC), and the year letter was 'A', he called that bull 'Abbott of Balmuick'. The next year was 'B', and the bull was called 'Bard of Balmuick', and so on, so he knew which year his bulls were born. 'Abbot' went to Mingary and 'Bard' to Glenfosa, 'Callum', from memory, to the Department of Agriculture fold at Loch Ness, but if I'm wrong I know some pedigree fanatic will put me right! 'Druid' was mistakenly castrated, but, as the old saying goes, 'if you want a good steer cut a good bull', and he won the Highland Cattle Championship at the Smithfield Fatstock Show. 'Ewen' went to Laudale and 'Fearacher' to a certain Ben Coutts at Gaskbeg. He was brought out to be Reserve Champion and Highest Priced Bull of the Year, at a huge three hundred and sixty guineas! I can't recall all the rest except for 'James' and 'John', the former going to Strathallan and the latter to Severie, where he produced some outstanding stock for many years.

To the ordinary reader the foregoing may well be boring reading, but oh! how we need Duncan's sort today: a dedicated stocksman, who was out to improve a breed, not destroy it as many have done for their own gain, and who was dead honest. Sadly, because he was so retiring he has never had the recognition that he should have had, and an OBE was but scant recognition of the job he did for the Shorthorn and Highland breeds, putting size into the former and flesh into the latter.

I got no joy trying to get Duncan interested in Highland ponies, although I know he did help his neighbour, 'Gillie' MacBeth of Dunira, with pedigrees. These years with DMS were the best schooling I ever had in my life, getting the benefit of his knowledge of pedigrees and how they should be used, while always remembering that there is a latent 'gene' (and don't we see that coming through in our families). How well his three 'grieves' nursed me along and gave me the deference I didn't deserve. And of course his cattlemen (and there were seven of them in those palmy days) were ungrudging in their advice and counsel. Duncan was taken by the old reaper far too early, in his fifties, but the Highland Cattle Society owe him a debt they will never be able to repay. So does the whole country, as he revitalised our native Highland breed. Apart from their value as exports, pictures of Highland cattle are used everywhere by the media, post-card firms etc. to promote the country and draw in the tourists. Sadly he never lived to see the breed's resurgence in the nineties.

However, much of the resurgence has been tied to the demand from overseas, which at the time of writing has dried up because of the threat of BSE. This really is a nonsense as far as hill cattle are concerned, as they should not be dependent on the sort of concentrate-feeding on which dairy cattle depend in the South-West of England, where the disease erupted. Another reason for the resurgence within this country is once again the looks of the cattle. People with money, and there seems to be a lot sloshing around in certain areas, who have an acre or two of land, often think the view would be enhanced with a Highland beast or two. Some become such pets that I wonder if they ever pay the supreme sacrifice! Duncan Stewart believed that the Highland cattle breed and the Galloways should be the basis of our beef industry. He thought they should be bred on the hills and their progeny crossed by an improving sire—the Beef Shorthorn in his day—should then go down to marginal farms and be crossed again by a terminal sire, the Aberdeen-Angus in his day (which thankfully has come back into favour again), with the final product being finished on arable farms. Sadly today all too many Highland folds are situated in good arable districts. The good land takes away a lot of the quality of the character of a Highland cattle beast's head, giving it a coarseness of horn, which is a pity, as after all Highland Cattle are famous for their looks.

I always remember the time I got Jock Gordon to Smithfield, which had been his life's ambition, but he had never been allowed because Duncan knew he would go on a 'spree'. I only got him there, as described in *Bothy to Big Ben*, on condition I kept him off the dram. Anyway, he had his very able sidekick with him, Sandy Gray. When I got there their beasts were unbrushed and Jock and Sandy were in the bar, whereas others were busy brushing, combing and oiling their beasts. When I remonstrated with them they very rightly pointed out, 'They've had a long journey, they've had some hay and water' (which was always brought from home, an essential thing especially in London where it is so chlorinated) 'and we'll get going on them in the morning.' How right and how wise, as the cattle that were being brushed and combed came out next day empty looking, whereas ours were rested and full. What super advice it was, and something I have remembered ever since. My pony club-daft daughters used to moan about taking heavy cans of water from home, until they saw other girls' ponies not drinking, and to their detriment.

There is no doubt that all cattle for shows and sales are brought out much better than they were before the last war. Shampoo, hairdriers (the latter so noisy that one can scarce hear oneself speak) etc. are used, and judging by the adverts for additives to feeds, one hasn't got a good show beast unless it had XYZ to eat beforehand! There is no doubt that certain families had a particular expertise at 'bringing out' cattle for show and sale. In the old days these families usually remained with one breed, and certain families were associated with the Highland breed—the Carmichaels, MacNabs, MacCallums, MacGillivrays and the MacPhails, to name but a few. However, when John Gordon moved from bringing out the Millhills' Shorthorns, with which he already had three Perth Bull Sale Champions, to bringing out Balmuick Highland bulls, he altered the whole scene. His secret was in the feeding. I don't know whether it started with the Scots cattlemen who went to the Argentine, or whether it was the Argentinians who gave the tip to the Scots, but over there they feed their bulls a wet mash of boiled barley and linseed (the latter with its oil puts a lovely shine on a beast's coat). The mash is almost like a thick soup. As John had used this on Shorthorns he did the same with his Highlanders, and the improvement was dramatic. Duncan Stewart's knowledge of pedigrees with his desire to put more flesh on Highland cattle, and John's ability to feed well were a terrific combination, and soon many of the top Highland cattle herdsmen were feeding their bulls better. Gone were the days when a bull, due to go to the Highland Show, was stood in a byre with its head tied to the 'trevises' on both sides so that it couldn't scratch out its hair, and stood up on top of a wooden pallet so that it didn't lie in its own urine!

I know I've recounted this story before but I always think a good story can stand re-telling. It was the year of the last big storm in 1947 (as I look out of the window in February, 1996, at eighteen inches of snow, this must be the next one!) 'Jock', as I called John Gordon, had been beaten for the championship, which would have been his third Highland Bull Sale Champion, yet his bull had still made the top price. We left Oban, where it was hard, hard frost, but we—Jock, Jock Burns (Jim Robert's cattleman at Strathallan) and yours truly—were in a lovely rosy glow thanks to all too much of 'John Barleycorn'. These were the days of First and Third Class on the rail, and Duncan Stewart and Sir James were up front in the First Class carriage. They were also the days of corridors on all coaches. As in Burns' 'Tam O' Shanter', we were:

> '…getting fou and unco happy
> We think na on the lang Scots miles
> …that lie between us and our hame.'

Because of our cheerful state we never noticed that as we travelled east there was snow, and by the time we got to Tyndrum, lots of it. Jock had been 'going his dinger' about the terrible judging he had suffered at the hands of Robert Inglis, the Atholl factor, who had been desk-bound during the war years and was out of touch with cattle. At this point, who should pass in the corridor, then seeing us, return and open the door, but Robert Inglis, whereupon Jock, turning round, said, 'I was just talking about you, Mr Inglis'. And Robert replied, 'How nice of you, Gordon,' little realising what Jock had been saying. That night Robert was, like many others, stuck in a snow drift, and it was weeks before he got his car home. I eventually got home thanks to a pony I borrowed from the Crieff Riding School, and when I enquired what would be the charge, I was told it would be the pony's keep until the snow melted. I had that damned animal until May! But is it a sure sign of old age on my part, or are the Jock Gordons of this world becoming fewer? Of one thing I'm certain, in my fifty years' connection with the Highland breed there have been tremendous changes, so in the next chapter let's look at them.

10

My Fifty Years in the Highland Cattle Breed

How things have changed since those halcyon days after the war when those of us who had been overseas fighting were simply glad to have got back alive. We looked on farming as a way of life, and though one had to make enough money to survive, money wasn't the be all and end all of life as it is today.

In the Highland cattle world there were many who had stuck by the breed through thick and thin, but times were changing and a lot of new breeders jumped on the bandwagon. This was partly because of the looks of the cattle: and as food, home-produced, was a priority just after the war, why not breed cattle you liked to look at every day? After serving for five hugely instructive years with Duncan Stewart I became tenant of a farm at Lagganbridge in Upper Speyside. When I went to Oban or Dingwall market I would see pen after pen of three- or four-year-old super Highland bullocks. Nowadays those pens will be full of cross continental bullocks that, although they mature earlier, will have cost much more to produce. Then, on the pedigree side, we had some folds with a big number of females. Looking back over the years, what an input the breed has had from the ladies (and this before the days of equal opportunity!)

Among the ladies in the years that I've been associated with the breed, there was Miss Turner of Kilchanaig who bred the sire of 'Fearacher of Gartlea', which did so much good to the breed immediately after the war. Then there was Miss Campbell Kilberry, our first lady president. We were way in front of other breed societies in realising the dedication ladies will give to the job, compared to all too many of the men who are too busy looking after their businesses to be bothered to do the amount of work required as a President of a Society. This is more true than ever in the nineties.

Then there was Mrs Chapman of Fanans, Taynuilt. When she had to disperse her fold they were walked through Glenlonan from Taynuilt. Alan MacKenzie, who had been manager at Fanans and had gone on to manage Ormsary, had been asked to come back to manage the 'drove'. He got hold of some of his 'drouthy cronies', of whom I was proud to be one, to help him. How I wish I had had a camera at the time, as that sort of exercise will never happen again. I was proud to be part of it, but how I would like to have had a photo of it and especially of those who took part. Half way through Glenlonan is Barguillean, and at that time the custodian was the great Highland cattle enthusiast Tommy MacDonald, of whom more later. Nothing would do but he would entertain us in true Highland fashion, after which the miles seemed shorter and it was a case of, as the song goes, 'Step we gaily on we go' etc. (until the drink died in us!)

Then among the other lady breeders was Mrs Douglas of Killilan, from whom I bought a bull named 'Spirag': he was one-eyed and because of that was always a bit twitchy, but he bred well. Then too there was Mrs Bobs de Klee, for whom I did an advisory job forty years ago. I always remember 'coling' hay (making wee stacks in the field) with her husband who had just retired from the army, and he was so proud of the first 'cole' that he built unaided, he sent Bobs to bring a camera and he and I were 'snapped' in front of it. 'Bobs' was one of Mull's great ladies, and I'm only sad she didn't live to see the great success that her son Murray, helped by Jimmy Laing, has made of the fold she loved. Rosemary Dalgleish only sold off in the nineties, having backed the breed through the lean years.

While I am talking about the ladies I should mention Mrs Hyde, Braes of Green-ock. Her husband Roger, as ex-C.O. of the Argylls, presented one of their Shetland ponies as a mascot to the regiment (which disgraced himself by rearing in front of the regiment's Royal Colonel in Chief!). When Roger died she put a   tremendous amount of work into their fold. The Hydes it was who came to my farm dispersal sale at Lagganbridge in 1959 and bought 'Muff of Laggan'. Muff was so named because Robbie McHardy, my shepherd and lifelong friend, came back after doing his round of the calving cows and remarked, 'Captain, you've got a super white calf out of the Douglas and Angus cow, it's a heifer and looks just like a lady's muff' (one of those things that warmed ladies' hands in the old days). So she was named 'Muff', and covered herself in glory, as she went from Braes of Greenock to Benmore where she bred the then record-priced bull in Oban in 1973 which was sold for two thou-sand, two hundred guineas, a fantastic price in those days. In her old age she was sold to Anne Baragh in Yorkshire, who is one of the Society's tremendous supporters. She in turn bred from her 'Angus Macdomhnull of Easton, which I was partly influential in getting Martin Leslie to buy as the Queen's stock-bull for the Balmoral Fold, where he did a good job producing three Oban Bull Championships.

Then, of course, Judy Bowser, who bought 'Muff' from the Braes of Greenock Fold, has been with the breed since the forties and is a great supporter as well as a past President. She would have been President for a second time, but I remember well Sir James Roberts, then in the chair, saying 'Mrs Bowser had agreed to be our next President, but as she's in calf we'll let her off the hook.' Some of the more sedate members of the Society were NOT amused. Lady MacRobert I have alluded to in another chapter.

In the last few years we have had so many lady breeders I would be unwise to name them or I'd miss some and be in terrible trouble, but I must mention Jane Nelson, Auchnacloich, who has graced the Highland cattle scene for more years than she (or I for that matter) would like to say. She took over the fold when her husband, Ernest, died and what a success story that has been. I know she'd be the

A photo of an historic occasion. Hector MacNeill, Secretary of State for Scotland, is seen here with the author, then manager for Ben Challum Ltd, on the day when the Hill Cow Subsidy was begun by the Labour Government, a subsidy which is enjoyed to this day

first to say how much she owes to the Burnies, MacGillivrays et al. that have helped her, but every fold needs a boss and Jane is now rightly the Society's only Honorary President.

Just after the war we had that lovely period when it was *de rigueur* to have a Highland cattle fold. In those days the Society had two dinners, one for the breeders and the other for the cattlemen. At the breeders could be, and usually were, the Dukes of Argyll and Montrose, the Earl of Mansfield, Lord Trent, Lord Lovat, Duncan McCallum, MP for Argyll, Major Gomme-Duncan, MP for Perth, Sir Charles MacLean of Duart (later to be Lord MacLean and Chamberlain to the Queen), Michael Noble, later to be Secretary of State for Scotland and Lord Glenkinglas, and Johnnie Bannerman, that lovely Scot, the Duke of Montrose's factor and later to be Lord Bannerman. What a star-studded lot they were, who all had influence in Westminster, and it was through that influence that Duncan Stewart, Sir James Roberts and McNair Snadden, MP for West Perth, the directors of Ben Challum Ltd., got the Hill Cow Subsidy through the then Labour Government, which hill farmers enjoy, rightly, to this day. I'm proud to own a photo of Hector MacNeill, the Labour Secretary of State for Scotland, and myself looking at the cross-Highland cows on a cold March day in Glenlochy, when the scheme was first put into effect. The thing I remember most about that day was not the lunch, as it might be if it had happened in the nineties, rather than the forties, for then Scottish hotels were 'gastronomic deserts' even more than some are today. No, it was the mishap of Sir Alec Glen, a lovely man, an habitual pipe smoker and head of the Department of Agriculture, in whose car he was driving me—no chauffeurs in those days. We were tail-end-Charlies in the convoy, and Sir Alec would keep trying to light his pipe while driving down the twisty glen road. Eventually the inevitable happened and we landed in the ditch. There were no tractors to pull one out then, so I had to run back to Kenknock and get Willie Hunter, the head shepherd, and his gang of shepherds, to push us out. We eventually arrived at the lunch about three quarters of an hour late, I mud-spattered and Sir Alec extremely embarrassed, as he was meant to have made the introductory speech!

In those days many Highland heifers were bought for crossing, and there were any amount of good Shorthorn bulls around to use as sires. I still believe the future of the breed depends on some breeders of store cattle doing this again, although sadly there are not so many good Shorthorn bulls available today, as they went through a bad stage. Just recently, however, one or two with a cross of Maine Anjou in their pedigree have been outstanding.

Just before the advent of BSE there was a terrific interest in Highland cattle from Europe, but back in the fifties the overseas interest was from the States and Canada. It was in 1953 when I was stewarding at the Smithfield Show in Earls Court, London, that an American (obviously so by his wide hat, broad belt, jeans which were almost unknown in this country then, and high heeled boots) approached me, as he had seen I was wearing the kilt, and ascertained that I was Vice-President of the Highland Cattle Society. His name was Leonard Pugsley and he said he wanted seven Highland yearling bulls, could I get them right away? The reason he wanted Highland cattle was that dwarfism was rife in the States in the fifties in the Angus and Hereford breeds, and he wanted a complete out-cross. I was to see examples of dwarfism on my Nuffield Scholarship visit there in 1959 and it was quite frightening, the cattle were the size of Dexters, and it was all brought about about by constant inbreeding.

As I had to be in the south all that week and Leonard only had a week in this country I phoned my President, Tommy MacDonald of Barguillean, Taynuilt. He was a super guy, an ex-navy DSC, who loved life and Scotland. He was the sort of laird Scotland could do with right now, but sadly he loved his fags and 'bamboozlers' too much and died all too young. 'Bamboozlers' were his drink, half sherry and half gin, and they certainly lived up to their name! Poor Leonard arrived in Taynuilt in a snowstorm, which his jeans couldn't cope with, and then he had to enjoy, but also endure, Tommy's hospitality. When I got home Tommy and I set about getting the seven bulls. I can honestly say that compared with what we were offered then we could get a miles better choice today, as then they were all of the 'hair and horn' brigade. At least they were all hard done, but not overdone, unlike today. They must have done some good, as Angus MacKay came back from a visit to the States in the nineties and said he had come across some of their progeny, so at least they could breed! Following this order Tommy was invited to go to the States and was given an order for twenty bulls, but by this time there were health problems for cattle exports to the USA.

1954 was a memorable year for me as I was elected President of the Society of this, to my mind, very special breed. Of all our Scottish breeds this the one that even a child brought up in a high rise flat in a city knows because of their majestic looks. Today of course the breed is used on all sorts of Highland adverts, postcards etc., although it does annoy me that some postcard manufacturers show bad specimens of the breed—even worse, I came across one postcard, cleverly trimmed, showing a Highland bull, which described it as 'a Highland Cow'! And I thought everyone in this day and age was clued up on sex, to judge by the amount shown on TV these days.

But back in 1954 being President of a Breed Society was a sinecure compared with today, when breed politics and in-fighting are the name of the game. My Vice-Presidents were two highly respected Scots, the first being Sir Charles MacLean (later Lord MacLean) of Duart, who had to give up when he became Chief Scout. 'Chips', as he was known, was the best after-dinner speaker it has been my pleasure to listen to. Then I had Michael Noble, who was to become not only a great friend but also MP for Argyll, Secretary of State for Scotland and finally Lord Glenkinglas. Sadly we don't get people of that calibre willing to do those sorts of unpaid jobs nowadays.

As it was fairly soon after the Second World War which because of various reasons, petrol rationing and labour shortage being the main ones, made contact between folds difficult, I decided in my year as President to instigate fold visits. The one I remember best was to Loch Avich, which is up a (then) ghastly one-track road from Taynuilt to Lochawe. As we de-bussed I could see that the fold, which wouldn't have seen a human being except their owner, Mr Smith, throughout all the war years, were not at all amused, and before all the members had clambered out of the bus the fold were high-tailing it over the nearest skyline! With a sigh Mr Smith said, 'Well, ladies and gentlemen, as there's not a fence between here and Lochawe [about three miles distant] you've seen my cattle, so come in and have a refresh.' End of fold visit.

I have mentioned how we had then as members of the Society some of the top aristocracy, but we also had some of the top 'Jocks'. There was the great occasion when the cattleman's dinner was held in one hotel and the official Society dinner in another. As Johnnie Bannerman, then factor for the Duke of Montrose, and I, small farmer and factor to one or two small estates, were neither 'fish nor flesh nor good red herring', we attended both. Johnnie was a super chap and a gifted Gaelic singer, and hugely popular at the herdsmen's supper, which in those days before TV had accordionists, fiddlers, singers and story tellers. One of the story-tellers, from Taynuilt, a Tyson, brought the house down and how I wish I'd written down some of his stories. After one of those cheery suppers a cattleman was found by the local 'polis' lying outside the Royal Bank. When woken up by the bobby he was asked why he was there. He replied, 'I kept knocking, but they wouldn't answer and let me in, and this is where I'm staying.' He thought when he saw the 'Royal' sign he was at the Hotel of the same name!

During my year as President I had some dealings with Lovat Fraser, the greatest auctioneer of pedigree stock of his day. Like his son Roley he was basically shy, which all too many thought was being snobbish. Anyway, Lovat got an order from a farmer in Lincolnshire for eight three-year-old Highland bullocks and passed it on to me, as I, through my association with Duncan Stewart, was the only member of the Highland Cattle Society he knew well. The Council, very rightly, decided they should be bought in Dingwall, as the East-coast cattle have more bone and substance compared with those in the West (thanks to the interminable rain!) and they told me to look after the order and make sure I did a good job. I must have succeeded in that, as I got a repeat order for five years (till I left Gaskbeg). I never had a letter, but always a cheque signed the day after the bullocks arrived. The repeat order would come through Lovat Fraser and to this day I don't know who the buyer was!

How I ever got the second order I'll never know, as after I bought the bullocks in Dingwall they had to stay for a week at Gaskbeg while I arranged a cattle truck for them from Dalwhinnie to Peterborough. Those were the days when one didn't clutter the roads with giant cattle and sheep lorries. One of the bullocks had a roving eye (but being a bullock not for the ladies) and always looked tetchy. I had organised quite a droving squad of eight to drive them over hill from Lagganbridge to Dalwhinnie, all experienced stocksmen, but they had one helluva job with this one beast. Instead of going over the bridge he decided it was quicker to go over the Spey. He should have been entered in the Grand National, judging by his jumping ability over normal stockproof fences and the bonnet of one car, and he could also have been a gardener judging by the number he got into. Thank goodness there were few in the Highlands in the fifties (I think I got away with three half-bottles of whisky to placate the owners). I was waiting at the station at Dalwhinnie, having gone in front, once the droving party had left the hamlet of Catlodge, the last habitation before Dalwhinnie. I had to make sure that there were sufficient gates etc. to make a funnel for the cattle to be syphoned into the truck. Luckily I had decided to have the cattle there three hours before take off, in case of emergencies. The cattle arrived half an hour before they were due to leave, and the wild steer made one last dash for freedom. Luckily he hit the top rail of the very high and substantial gates the stations used to keep for loading cattle, turned a somersault and winded himself. As his head was facing the door of the truck we all leapt on him and shoved him in, whereupon the rest followed and up went the door just as the shunting engine came in to join the truck to the rest of the goods train.

As we were having our 'nip and chasers' (whisky and a half pint of beer) in Duggie Matheson's pub (one of the super old Highland landlords, sadly no longer with us) and I'd paid the bill for at least three rounds, I was thinking, well, that's the most expensive non-event I've ever been responsible for. That bullock will take off, join the local hunt, take every jump in sight, end of deal. But no, up came the cheque, no complaints and repeat orders. Would it were always thus!

As I said at the start of this chapter, when I was a Breed Society President it was in the palmy days when folk were recovering from the war and many farmers, hill farmers especially, looked on their calling as a way of life as well as a means of making a living. Nowadays farming is a business and big business at that. The result is that breed societies now are run by business-minded people, and they expect their Secretaries to be similarly minded.

In my Presidential year my Society Secretary was a Dunblane lawyer called Stewart. He was known locally as 'Swicky' Stewart ('swicky', to my sassenach readers, is Scots for dishonest, and nothing could be further from the truth). The only thing I held against him during our very happy year's association was the occasion at a breed function in Oban when we had to share a bedroom, and he wouldn't allow me to open a window. His 'combinations', which older men wore in these days, normally only by day, he kept on to sleep in, and they didn't smell of sweet violets! I always remember him telling me we had to make more money if the Society was to stay solvent, and against fierce opposition at the AGM, as heifers were selling well, we managed to get the herd book entry charge for heifers changed from seven and sixpence up to ten shillings, big deal. It's rather fun looking back over the years and re-reading one's pronouncements, whether in print or on the air, and I was a lucky laddie to be given a lot of airtime on the radio in the fifties and sixties. I found one I'm proud of from when I was President, after there had been a groundswell of opinion that we should be thinking of the beef potential of the breed and not its looks. I'm reported as saying, 'A breed is dying when one stops trying to improve it, and so our breed is far from dead, as everyone seems to have ideas on how to improve it.'

Sadly, nowadays, in all breeds of stock, all too many are thinking of personal profit instead of what is good for the breed as a whole. If you doubt me, just look back at what happened to the Beef Shorthorn and Aberdeen Angus breeds in those halcyon years after the war, when they pandered to the mighty dollar of the States and the more than useful pesos of the Argentine, and bred the wee dumpy bulls that those countries wanted. In so doing they neglected their home breeders who wanted longer, stretchier cattle. What worries me about the Highland cattle breed is that it will increasingly be taken over by breeders who have a lot of money and can employ a first-class stocksman (which I've seen happen all too often in other breeds with which I've been associated) but forget that these cattle, the oldest breed in Scotland, are meant to be bred to survive on the sort of pastures I mentioned in a previous chapter about Uist. Yes, they were great days to be President of a breed Society as life moved at a slower pace then and communications were not so good. As a result one didn't have irate breeders writing or phoning about problems they thought the Society ought to sort out, which I understand is the norm today and a President and a Secretary's nightmare.

One of the nice things I had to do in my Presidential year was to find a stock bull for the Corriemuchlock fold belonging to Sir William Rootes (later Lord) of 'Hillman

'Shaun of Laggan', Highland Cattle Champion at Smithfield in 1957, one of the many Highland steers sold by the author in the fifties to Yorkshire

Imp' fame. Luckily I'd seen a really good fleshy bull in the Black Isle belonging to Major Shaw-Mackenzie. This bull was 'Alastair Rhuadh', bred at the Douglas and Angus Estate by Mr MacLaren the factor, who had his own fold as well. That bull was the kind that then was hard to find, and today what a lot of breeders would like to have him. He had a good masculine head, he was right on his legs, with plenty of bone, well fleshed and could move, and luckily he was for sale!

One of the many other nice things in my Presidential year was to see a steer of my breeding, 'Shaun of Laggan', win the Highland Cattle Championship at the Royal Smithfield Show. That year was also very special for me, as the Supreme Champion of the Show, 'Highland Princess' (a cross Shorthorn-Aberdeen Angus heifer), was also bred at Gaskbeg. Incidentally, she was led on this occasion by a wee laddie called Jim Stobo, who is now chairman of umpteen committees, President of the Royal Smithfield Club, one of the trustees of the Queen Mother's Castle of Mey Estate and in reward for all his many public duties, rightly, wears the CBE.

What led to 'Shaun' winning the Highland Championship was my meeting with a super Yorkshireman called Pearson Brown during my time as junior Vice-President two years before. Pearson was to be a close friend of mine until his premature death. He was a butcher of the old sort, of which there are all too few today. He it was who showed to me how tasty beef should be prepared. He got his cattle that were to be slaughtered into one of those old round buildings that pre-war were used to grind

'Rory o' More of Laggan', First Prize Junior Steer at Smithfield, 1959. The last animal —and the last winner!—to be shown by the author before he gave up the tenancy of Gaskbeg

oats, with a horse going round and round to turn the mill stones. As these buildings were no longer needed, because of water and electric power, people used them for different things. Pearson used his for housing his cattle (in semi-darkness) for a day. The cattle were driven in on a Saturday night and were left there quietly, as no one worked in those days on Sunday, were gently walked down a race on Monday morning and were humanely killed on the same day. As Pearson always said to me all those forty-plus years ago, 'Ben, they haven't been stressed, so the adrenalin isn't working'. Then he hung the carcasses for at least ten days (he used to say that they ought to hear the church bells twice!) Oh! how I wish the modern supermarkets would see that their suppliers followed old Pearson's ways of doing things. Nowadays the cattle are bashed into lorries, bashed into marts, bashed into slaughter-houses then hung up and put into supermarkets within the next two or three days from slaughter, with a red glow about the newly slaughtered beef that the modern housewife seems to want. She couldn't be more wrong: if she wants something tender that has a real taste about it, it ought to be mahogany colour.

Pearson introduced me to a Mr Hughes, a Yorkshire feeder of beef cattle who bought Highland bullocks to finish, and two he bought from me won the Highland Cattle Championship at Smithfield, 'Mulach' and 'Shaun'. Pearson was the person who put Highland cattle on the map in Yorkshire. He it was who got the Yorkshire Show directors to include Highland cattle classes in their Show which I, wearing all different sorts of hats, think is the best show in Great Britain. Everyone you meet there asks you, 'What do you think of *our* Show?' They all back it and it hasn't got too big. As for Highland cattle breeders I'll bet they'll tell you that the Yorkshire and Dalmally are their favourite shows. If I'm right Pearson and I had more than friendship in common, as he instigated Highland cattle at the former and I at the latter show. He achieved something no other Highland cattle breeder has a 'ghoster of a chance' of doing nowadays, in that he had a Highland bullock in the final line up of four for the overall Championship at Smithfield in 1938. This is when older cattle were still wanted, whereas since the last war the final line up for the Championship has been from the suckled calf and yearling classes.

I little thought in the period 1953 to 1954, when Michael Noble was at home running his and his brother's estate, because it was in their joint ownership, that (a) we would become such good friends and (b) that I would be asked to go to manage the estate. When the latter happened in 1959 I found the Highland cows in a byre at Clachan, where some readers may have enjoyed an oyster lunch in the nineties! The first thing I did, having had to milk the old cow that had too much for its calf, was to the kick the lot out to live as Highland cattle are meant to do. I'm proud to say that in the five years I was there we won the Female Championship at the October Sales in Oban not once but twice. It gave me great pleasure when I went back to Clachan Oyster Bar after all these years to write in the visitor's book, 'I'd rather tuck in than muck out at Clachan'—no exaggeration, because when I was milking those Highland cows (all marvellous kickers) and the cattleman was ill I was the one who had to muck out the byre! Who would be a factor when you are the only one on the estate who could milk a cow? Or at least the only one willing to admit he was be able to do it?

When I came to Woodburn in 1964 I kept a few Highlanders but it wasn't easy mixing them with my cross-Highland cows which were of course polled, and it wasn't easy to run two units of cows as I had done at Gaskbeg. As prices for Highlands were depressed at that time it made sense to stick to the cross-cattle, as I had a second family to educate! However I did keep my hand in by bringing out the odd beast, and won the yearling heifer championship twice at the October Sales, once with one of mine and once with one from Glenartney.

Now we have seen a fantastic resurgence in the breed. BSE has momentarily halted the European demand but the home demand is still strong for good cattle. The type of owner has changed completely in the last fifty years. The names that I mentioned at the beginning of this chapter are few and far between and have been replaced by many who have only recently become country-dwellers. Now, sadly, we have fewer breeders who are practical farmers and know their stock and how to feed and handle them.

I little thought when I was President in 1954 that I would live to hear a breeder get up at an AGM and say he was going to take out a legal injunction against the Society because he wasn't getting his own way in how he felt the Society's sale should be run. I've seen his kind before, and he lasted only two years in the breed as his motion was heavily defeated!

The Highland pony scene has gone through its own momentous changes in the last fifty years, and these are the subject of my next chapter.

11
Highland Ponies and Breeders
after the 1939–45 War

After the Second World War, like all breeders of pedigree stock, Highland pony breeders had almost to start from scratch. Few ponies were registered during the war years, but there were some established studs which had some superb mares. George Baird, who had always from his early farming days known what a good horse should look like, took a farm near Perth and set up one of the outstanding studs of recent times with the suffix of 'Whitefield'. George realised how important some of the old bloodlines were, and in 1965 when the Derculich ponies were for sale, George, who knew a good thing when he saw it, went up there with his son, one in the Land Rover and one in the lorry. When the Land Rover came home with nothing in the trailer, Mary, George's wife, thought nothing had been bought, but later in came the lorry with seven on board, and three with foals at foot—all bought for nine hundred pounds, a shrewd buy. 'Mayfly of Derculich', which won the Highland Show, was not one of that lot. She was bought privately, and sadly she lost twins in 1970.

George always, and rightly, pulls my leg about a piece of business I had with him in the fifties. He had a horse, 'Glengarry III', bred by my old friend Duncan Lamont, Invervack, Blair Atholl, and off it I had a super colt foal when I was in Gaskbeg. I sent our Deparment-bred mare to him from Woodburn, and she bred a black foal. As George had one or two stallions standing at Whitefield at that time I stupidly asked him, 'Are you sure this foal is by Glengarry?' I had never seen a black foal off the old horse before, and as they say, 'It's a wise man who knows his own father'. It would be hard to prove, but suffice to say it was one of the best horses Sal and I ever had. It came home to Woodburn having been ridden by Sal to win the Highland Pony Ridden Class at Perth Show, only to be found dead the next morning with the dreaded grass sickness.

George always wanted to have the best, and not only bought from Derculich but also from Meggernie, Drumloist, whose owner, Mrs Barr, was a Cairns, a famous name in the Highland pony world. Jimmy Cairns was of the West Biggs near Blackford, a north-facing hill farm, the like of which I wouldn't like to farm. It must be good for stock on those farms on the north side of the Ochil hills, however, as Bardrill was next door, where Messer and Pete Sharp did more than well with their Clydesdales. It was back in 1908 that Jimmy Cairns bought his first Highland pony, and he founded a famous family which he called the 'Calliach Bhan' (the white-haired lady). These went on up to Calliach Bhan XXII with Jimmy; but there is a nice photo of his daughter 'Babs' Mackenzie showing Calliach Bhan XXVI, a twelve-year-old mare, at an Aberdeen Show in 1991. Some family (both the Cairns and the Calliach Bhans!) and how long-lived both families are! Jimmy died in his nineties.

He was one of the last of the 'gentlemen farmers' that it has been my pleasure to know. Living in the days when labour was plentiful and cheap, there was little need for them to do physical work. They were always impeccably dressed, in his case with a deer-stalker bonnet, plus-four suit, ghillie brogues polished so you could see your face in them, and of course, always a tie, a fair change from the dress some farmers wear today! Also they always had excellent manners and could converse with the highest in the land and those not so fortunate.

Jim was one of the Cairns family who rented the island of Luing from the Earl of Breadalbane. After the war the island was taken over by the Cadzow brothers, Shane, Dennis and Ralph, and as they were about to stock it with cross-Highland heifers bred in Glenlochay, which I then managed, they asked me over to stay. Two things I will never forget about that visit in the late forties. One was seeing the old byre, built in a square, which held one hundred cows tied by the neck—yes, one hundred: just imagine the labour it took to milk and muck out that lot. The Cadzow brothers found that the building, with its wooden standings, was so full of T.B. that they decided to out-winter their cows. These are now accepted as the 'Luing' breed. The second thing I remember was buying lobsters from the local fisherman at one pound each, and they were big beauties too. Sadly the French found out how good they were and they can't be bought locally any more.

Anyway, the Cairns family in their days in Luing were good supporters of the Highland pony breed, and 'Donald of Luing' was the grandsire of two well-known stallions, 'Drambuie' and 'Glengarry III'. When Jimmy died he was the last surviving founder-member of the Highland Pony Society. So, with all that background to his stock, it was no wonder George Baird had to include some Calliach Bhans in his stud.

Judging by the photos one sees of the Calliach Bhans they were good middle-of-the-road types, between the heavier garrons and the lighter-legged Western Isles type. For my taste I would like to have seen more breed character in them: they didn't seem to have that classic Highland pony head that I like—slightly dished, small pricked ears, real breadth between the eyes and with big nostrils. George's ponies always looked a bit long in the head for my liking, but who am I to criticise? My judgement has been questioned many times, and by none more strongly than by George Baird when he was judging the females and I the males at the Highland Show. My male Champion was an eight-year-old stallion, and had to my mind all the things a Highland pony should have: presence, a wonderful mane and tail (essential to brave the cauld blasts we have in Scotland) and he could move straight. George reckoned he was too small for his age, but right from my pony-boy days I never wanted a big one with a long back, which as in humans can give a lot of

'Viscount of Whitefield' from George Baird's famous stud (Alan Baird)

problems, nor did I want to have to load a stag onto anything bigger than I had to! However I was more than willing to give way to George's female Champion mare, but was not amused when the umpire put up the female Reserve Champion as overall Reserve Champion. I was more than pleased when my Champion went on to greater things in England, where perhaps they are not so restricted in their views or so worried about who bred the beast.

But one time I do know George agreed with my judgement was at Turriff Show, when I made one of the many lovely mares with the Whitefield suffix Champion. This is one of the shows where all the judges of the different main sections, horses, cattle and sheep have to confer to decide which is to be the overall Champion of each section. I kept telling the other judges in my section, of Shetlands, Clydesdales, Hunters, Mountain and Moorland etc., how good George's mare was, and the result didn't, for once, do me any harm in George's estimation. George is one of the dedicated breeders who built a super stud on the best lines he could find, and if he made a penny or two on the way, then jolly good luck to him say I, as there are very, very few who make money from pedigree livestock.

I am glad to say he has passed on his interest to his sons, and one of them, Alan, lent me a stallion card of the kind which were common pre-war, of 'Beinn Odhar', bred by the Duke of Atholl. This horse was Champion at the Inverness Highland in 1923, and he was standing at Auchenleck Killearn at three pounds and three shillings service fee. The groom's fee was five shillings, which would be one eighth of his weekly wage in those far-off days. The Whitefield suffix, which is seen everywhere nowadays, and rightly so, because of the thought that has been put into purchasing the best blood procurable, will be carried on by George's sons. The nicest thing that I could say about George has been bettered by someone who, after George's presidency of the Society, wrote: 'He was honest, helpful, unassuming and graced the position with dignity and moderation, always helped in the background by his wife, Mary'. And so say all of us. (Sadly, since I penned the above, George has passed on, but he got a terrific send-off, with one of the biggest funeral turn-outs seen in Perth for many years.)

On Tuesday, 13 December 1977, the Knocknagael stud of Highland ponies were sold off in Inverness, which was one of the worst things that ever happened to the Highland Pony Society. Jimmie Dean, whom I wrote up in my book *Auld Acquaintance* and for whom I had a tremendous regard, ruled the roost from there in the north as far as the Department of Agriculture was concerned, as it was from there that they hired out stallions, bulls and rams, which all did a great job in improving the stock throughout the Highlands and Islands, especially in the crofting townships. There are many super crofters whom I can call friends, but I must say that when it came to choosing a sire for their cows, mares or ewes, as long as it had four legs and the two essentials that Squeaky Robertson told those loading the bull on Rhum to look after, the crofters didn't mind about anything else. So this is where the Department did a super job. Of course they were criticised, but I had a lot of time for Jimmie and his team, who were real stocksmen and impartial. As I write this chapter I have in front of me the catalogue of the Knocknagael stud dispersal, which states that it is the result of a 'change of policy' in the Department of Agriculture for Scotland. How often in my lifetime in farming have I heard the dreaded words 'change of policy', seldom, if ever, for the better. On the front of the catalogue is a photo of 'Glenmuick', to my mind exactly what a Highland pony should look like.

Looking through the catalogue one finds that 'Glen Aigus', born in 1976 and so now twenty-one years old, was bought by none other than Liz Compton (née Cox), who has done so much for the breed. Liz was, like me, employed on the Strathallan Estate in Perthshire at the end of the war, when I was managing some farms there and she was a land girl. The Estate was famous for its stock seed potatoes, and its owner, Sir James Roberts, was accepted as one of the most knowledgeable of Scottish seed potato growers. These potatoes had to be inspected by students who had been trained to do the job. They came round, of course, even then, with copious forms that had to be filled in. I remember well on one occasion that a squad bossed by an ex-Royal Engineer wounded officer came into the lunch which we always provided. We had always wondered why the inspection squads came in nice time to inspect the tatties and finish just in time for lunch. All was revealed when the squad went to the loo, leaving their form on my desk, and on the top was written 'Jolly good grub here'. The sequel to this story is that the leader of that particular gang, John Compton, married Liz Cox, and has helped her since then to give endless hours, days, months and years to the promotion of Highland ponies. Liz, whom I have now known for fifty-two years, has given invaluable service not only to the Highland Pony Society, of which she has been a Council member from 1960 to 1996, and its President, but has represented the Highland Pony Society on the National Pony Society from 1970 to 1991, a fair record of commitment by one person, and I know from my own experience how much time and money these appointments can cost one.

She, like me, was a tremendous admirer and supporter of the Department of Agriculture ponies and of Jimmie Dean. She has used stallions bred by the D.O.A.S. or their offspring for forty-six years, and is now wondering where to go for the outcross that can either 'nick' (as we say in the livestock world) or ruin one's stock. There's also an old saying that when you use males and females that are closely bred, and if you happen to breed a 'good un', that's called 'line breeding', but that if it turns out to be a runt it's 'in-bred'.

Jimmie Dean always said he wanted 'to breed ponies to move', which is why Liz liked the Department bloodlines, as all too many breeders just after the war might as well have been showing pigeons or canaries at a show, as their ponies were never being used for riding, driving or for their original job, working on hill farms and

'Gipsy Meg of Turin Hill', Liz Compton's favourite mare, which won the coveted Royal Highland Show Championship in 1974. She looks the part, with presence, depth of rib, good flat bone and a good hock (Mrs J.C. Compton)

estates. This, I'm glad to say, has now changed, and nowadays the demand for ponies for riding is fantastic. Usually they have to be broken and quiet, as the majority of buyers just want them for hacking around the countryside, if they are lucky enough to live in an area where there is any of it left! The breed's ability to be out-wintered with but little feed is ideal for the weekend rider.

Liz had an aunt in Glenshee who fired her love for the breed. This aunt owned the 'Lord of the Isles', bred in 1919, who was sired by 'Bonnie Laddie', a well known sire—and what super names they gave their ponies in those far-off days, they sound as if they could do their mares a bit of good! Liz bought her first mare from the great Donald Lamont (a great pin-up of mine, and like Jimmie Dean, in *Auld Acquaintance*). The mare was called 'Shanter's Maggie', and cost one hundred pounds in 1952, a lot of money then before the awful decimalisation which put everything through the roof. Liz reckons it was her best investment ever, as although the mare died of the dreaded 'grass sickness' (for which as I write in 1996 there has been no cure found) three weeks after producing a filly foal, the foal, 'Tam o' Shanter's Meg', was hand-reared and was the grandmother of 'Gipsy Meg of Turin Hill'. The latter, whose photo you see on the opposite page, was Champion of the Royal Highland Show in 1974. With 'Glenmuick', these are the sort of Highland ponies that I would like to have bred myself, but sadly, I never had the time nor the ability. Liz had another good mare, 'Bog Myrtle of Turin Hill', who produced seventeen foals in seventeen years without a break. When you compare this with the terrible problems the thoroughbred breeders have even getting some mares in foal, and I came across this way back in the late thirties when I worked as a groom in one of the top thoroughbred studs in the country, you can see how much the ponies of Great Britain have got to give to the horse scene in the world.

Liz has not only done her bit for the breed, but has also bred a daughter, Margaret, who has ridden five Highland pony Champions in the ridden classes at the Royal Highland Agricultural Show. Her mother judged these classes in 1992, a high honour, but needless to say Margaret was not showing on that occasion.

Judging these big shows is a nightmare, as one knows some of the competitors personally, also one is on one's own with a crowd of critical onlookers (I was the best rugby player Scotland ever had, on the touchline) and it's never easy to decide, as there may be ponies, cattle or sheep in front of you that have been winning at show after show because XYZ made them Champion on their first show appearance. At subsequent shows judges don't want to question the great man/woman's judgement, so although they may have an animal in front of them that hasn't yet been confronted by the reigning 'champ', they are not sure what to do and go for the animal favoured by XYZ. As in all walks of life it's not 'what you know' but 'who you know'. Sadly, in stock-judging, it is summed up as far as I'm concerned by a great pal of mine who bred Clydesdale horses and had loved showing at all the Scottish shows. A year or two ago I met him, I think it was at Ayr, which always used to have a good entry of Clydesdales. I said to him, 'Jock, why are you not showing?' and the answer was terse. 'Weel, Ben, you see a' my judges are deid.' The

The author judging the working Highland pony class at the Breed Show, 1996
(the McArdles)

aforesaid is not to say that judges are crooks, far from it, but the standard of show-manship these days is so high that often one is left with the dilemma of having two animals in front of one with prctically nothing to choose between them. One is led by a friend/acquaintance. Does one favour the person or be hard on him/her? It's often a difficult decision to make.

Along with Liz a number of established breeders attended the Knocknagael Stud dispersal, among them George Baird, Lady Swinton, Bill Merchant, Mary McCall-Smith as she was then (now Mrs MacPherson) who breeds the famous high-priced Blackface sheep, both tups and ewes, the MacIntoshes and Bert Macrae the vet. The latter and I have something in common in that we entered the old Glasgow Veteri-nary College together and had as a mate a certain Alfie Wight. Bert and Alfie passed their exams and became vets. I on the other hand failed mine brilliantly and became a groom instead, but thanks to the war, managed to pull myself up by my shoe laces! Alfie became better known as James Herriot and died a millionaire. Bert is still going strong, is as besotted with his Highland ponies as ever and takes grazing all over the place to feed his ever increasing stud.

Another great supporter just after the war was Mrs Davidson, otherwise known as Mittie, with her Trowan stud near Crieff. She was born a McAra, and her father was well known for driving a Highland pony to Crieff market every Tuesday and hitching it to the railings in St James Square. Oh, how I wish we could do that today, instead of having to cross the road in fear and trembling while the drivers of huge lorries, buses and four-wheel-drive vehicles vie with each other as if they were trying to be like Damon Hill! I had the honour of making Mittie's black Highland pony mare Champion at a Crieff show over forty years ago. The mare went on to be Champion at the R.H.A.S. and then to found a dynasty of good ponies at Trowan, now looked after by Mittie's son Robert, who is a great enthusiast.

The suffix of 'Kinmonth' started in the twenties, when the ponies were registered by J. Moncrieff-Wright, but for most of us the name relates to Lt. Col. D.G. Moncrieff who was such a super supporter of the breed. His daughter, Mrs Heather Gow, has not only done her stint on Council and been President, but has been a great and enthusiastic member and specialised in breaking and driving Highland ponies. As she now owns the Moncrie-ff estate in the north she has changed the suffix from 'Kinmonth' to 'Alltnacailleach'. Heather it was who kindly lent me the family stud book, which makes wonderful reading for an oldie like me. The ninth entry in the stud book fascinated me, as 'Sybil of Kinmonth', born in 1932, had as her grandsire 'Ronald II', the stud horse in Glenartney, which eventually was castrated to go down the mines. I doubt if such a thing would be allowed today—what a pathetic end to a horse who had left his mark on the Highland pony breed, and how sad that someone as wealthy as the Earl of Ancaster would allow it to happen (or perhaps, once again, it was the Factor's decision?)

At the beginning of the stud book was enclosed a letter from the Factor of Rhum, written in 1964, confirming that the stud horse 'Diabhiah of New Calgary', a six-year-old, would be delivered to Mallaig for the price of sixty pounds—but that Col. Moncreiff would need to pay for his transport to Perth! Isn't it strange how

'Skye of Alltnacailleach' being driven through the water hazard at the Scone Scottish Driving Championships by his owner Heather Gow. He was ridden at the Royal Highland Show to win that Championship, thus illustrating the versatility of the breed (Heather Gow)

we've got used to the 'new' money after decimalisation and inflation? When I showed the letter to a young modern breeder she couldn't believe it, and said, 'That price wouldn't pay its fare now from Rhum to Mallaig'.

There is no doubt that the outstanding animal bought for the Kinmonth Stud was 'Isle of Arran Bonnie Jean'. Although she was bought from the Duke of Montrose, who of course then owned a large slice of the island, the mare was bred at Balmoral by George V, so why she had an Isle of Arran prefix beats me.

Heather was brought up in Kinmonth, and remembers her first pony, which was 'Stella of Kinmonth', a six-year-old in 1965 and got by 'Seoras of New Calgary'. Stella bred 'Stephanie', who was by an Arab, as Heather was in the south of England in the sixties and Highland pony stallions were few and far between there in those days. 'Stephanie' was an outstanding Pony Club performer, and like her mother before her was still going strong at the age of twenty! But since Heather and her husband Jock moved back north to Pitscandly, her association with 'Skye', another daughter of Stella's, has resulted in numerous wins in driving competitions. Heather has been one of the few in the Highland Pony Society since the last war to extol the virtues of the breed for working purposes, as she not only has good driving ponies but also has them carrying deer on her estate in the north. The Society could do with many more like her. The Kinmonth Stud was certainly left in a safe pair of hands.

Sal and I bought a pony from Heather more years ago than I care to remember. This pony was named 'Dionard of New Calgary': she was a topper, and is still going strong winning riding classes, although well into her twenties, for Mrs Hoad in England. When we got her home Sal had her broken to the trap, and they were taken on as extras in the film *Chariots of Fire*. The scene they were in was being shot on the haugh above the Newton Bridge in the Sma' Glen. The hill above the bridge is known to the Coutts family as 'Calgers' hill for the following reason. The scene to be shot was of Eric Liddell competing in the local Highland Games: surrounding the arena were ponies and traps, among which were Sal and 'Calgers', our pet name for Dionard. Those of you who have ever taken part in a film or a T.V. recording will know just how boring they can be. The director says ad infinitum, 'That was great, but we'll just take another shot', and so it goes on all day—'Take one', 'Take two', 'Take three' etc. etc. Not only was Calgers brassed off with the tedium of standing still for hours, she did not like the starting-pistol used for the races one little bit, and even in the final shot which was eventually in the completed film, if you happen to see it, the pony that starts back is you know who!

After the boring day they'd had, Sal decided to let the pony have a graze before I was due to pick them up at the bridge. Sal, obviously as a result of also being bored stiff and tired, let Calgers go without a head collar on, most unlike my usual efficient horse handler, whereupon Calgers started to graze on up the hill. Every time Sal got near her the mare moved on, and there's not a fence on that hill till one comes to Corriemuchloch, three miles distant! Eventually, after following Calgers for forty minutes Sal got her caught, but it was a tired pair that I fetched home from Newton Brig' that night, and they had earned their film-appearance money. So Calgers is famous for two things, first for appearing in a well-known film and second because she is still winning ridden classes when many would think she would be past her sell-by date.

Talking of being famous for two things reminds me of my good friend, Geordie Scott, who managed the Glenalmond Estate for the late Lord Rootes. Geordie lived at Corriemuchloch, just mentioned, and this was in the days before one fed hill sheep with feeds made up in lick blocks. In his day, in time of storm a hill farmer fed his ewes with hay bought from the Carse of Stirling, which was baled then with wire. It was baled out of the stack, and was lovely hay, but was held by wire and the bales weighed about a hundredweight. So, like polythene string on farms today, which at least for all its smell you can burn, there was always a fair amount of baling wire knocking about. Geordie's great remark to me when I said how well his cast ewes had sold in Perth was, 'Aye, Ben, but Corriemuchloch's only famous for two things, baling wire and empty bottles'. So perhaps that is why Calgers, who was famous for two things, puts me in mind of Corriemuchloch!

12

Highland Ponies and Cattle
in England

There is no doubt that people in England were the first to realise that the Highland pony could do more than just be a crofter's best friend, to pull a cart, work on the land, and be hired out to a grouse moor in August/September to help pay the rent. From the beginning those down south who bought the ponies wanted to ride or drive them or both. As I warned in my Acknowledgements at the beginning of the book, I'm not going to be able to mention in this chapter all too many who have been supporters of the breed south of the border, but for various reasons, in my humble opinion, there are some whose work for the breed stands out from the rest.

To me one of the great characters in the breed in the south was the late Miss Wilby, who founded her stud Nashend in 1944 with a pony bought from Devon to hoe the turnips. By the time Clive and Penny Smith were employed to help out in 1967 there were eighty ponies, of which five were stallions. But long before Miss Wilby had made her mark in breeding Highland ponies she had done many other things. She was a great rally driver, and always in Fraser Nash cars—which were, to any younger readers, a very famous British pre-war make. She bought Nashend in 1947 after war service in the MTTC (Mechanised Transport Corps). Miss Dobson, Miss Wilby's partner, had lived in the area before the war and was also a great stock enthusiast.

Lest any reader think that there was more in the friendship of these two grand old ladies than meets the eye, I should mention that Miss Eddie (as Miss Dobson was known) had been a 'Bluebell girl', and Miss Wilby said she loved the men, but would never marry because any man she married would have less money than she had, and she couldn't put up with that. (Her sale of Nashend, lock, stock and barrel, in 1985, made three hundred and sixty-five thousand pounds, and there was a million or two more in shares!) But the two old ladies must have known quite a bit about stock breeding, as they successfully bred Nashend Royal's 'Gay Lady' which held the record, in the world, for the quantity of milk produced by a Jersey cow.

Then they set about breeding Highland ponies to ride and drive. Being in the Beaufort Hunt country they made certain that Nashend ponies were seen at the Meets, and the cry used to go up, 'Let's breach that hedge, where are the Highlands?' Thanks to Clive and Penny Smith, who are avid hunt supporters in and out of the saddle, Highland ponies are still seen out with the Beaufort—though these days the more modern type of pony can jump better and they don't need to 'breach the hedge'.

In 1957 the Nashend Stud sent a mouse dun stallion to Pakistan, about as far 'Furth of Scotland' as it is possible to get! The horse was to be used in an experiment of crossing stallions of different breeds of British ponies with the native donkey jennies, to see which cross produced the best mule. Of the breeds used, which must have included Welsh, Welsh Cob, Dales, New Forest et al., the Highland cross was acclaimed the best. I hope when all those awful Afghanistan problems are sorted out, the Pakistan Government will come back for more stallions to produce that wonderful animal, the mule. During the Sudan-Eritrea-Abysinnian campaign in 1940, as an ex-groom, I was put in charge of a supply company who used mules for their transport and in my opinion no pure breed of horse or pony, and I mean NO breed, would 1) carry their loads, 2) live on as little feed and water, but 3) be as bloody awkward as could a mule!

Nashend's name has continued to flourish thanks to Penny and Clive, and they have had standing at stud 'Balmoral Dee', which was broken and handled by the McArdles at Denmill for Her Majesty, and 'Dee' is now being hunted with the Beaufort! Like many well known studs they have taken advantage of the recent overseas demand for Highland ponies. They have sent ponies to Holland which have done well, but they both reckon that 'Nashend Sea Storm', which won the NPS award at the Highland Show, was the best they've bred—as Clive said, 'You could ride him on a finger'. What a recommendation for any horse!

Lady Norah Fairfax-Lucy, whom I have already mentioned in my Mull chapter, had a tremendous influence on the promotion of the breed in England. It's sad that to this day there is an undercurrent of north versus south as far as the breed is concerned, and Norah was right in the middle of it. Being very much the daughter of her father Munro-Mackenzie of Calgary she favoured the Western Isles type, and was influential in encouraging the South West Peninsula Highland Pony Breeders, located in the South West of England—which had, according to one well known breeder, been formed out of the ashes of the South of the Border Association of Breeders! It's so sad that all breed societies have those terrible internal feuds, but believe me it still goes on, though of that more later. Norah had to disperse her stud after the premature death of her husband in 1944, and her good stallion 'Dune' (named after the only wee hill in Iona) went to Sir Alfred Goodson, one of the greatest stocksmen I've been fortunate to know.

Every breed of stock he bred were the tops. The hounds in his College Valley pack, that he hunted, are to this day sought after by breeders of hounds in the Shires who want hounds with the speed and stamina which are characteristic of those raised on Border hills. His 'Eulima' female line of Aberdeen-Angus constantly won the female championships at the Highland Show. I remember well back in 1950, when I was the then trainer of the Young Farmers Club Scottish Beef judging team going to Kilhan at Mindrum. 'Bill' Goodson (as he was affectionately known) had this cow paraded in front of the team and declared, 'There's what you want to look for, she has a head like a housemaid and an arse like a cook.'

Then, too, his flock of Cheviots were famous, as were his fighting cocks. Just after the war he and my then boss, Duncan Stewart of Millhills, used to have an annual 'main' i.e. a match of so many cocks. As it was even then unlawful, Bill kept his fighting cocks in pens behind the hound kennels, so that if anyone was snooping the hounds gave a warning. Duncan had his on one of his hill farms. I had to cart the cocks to wherever the main was to be held. Looking back, it was amazing to see two of the greatest stocksmen this country has produced engrossed in cockfighting, but they didn't do it for the joy of seeing the spectacle: it was because they reckoned that to breed a champion fighting cock was harder to do than to breed a champion bull, ram, hound or, Bill said, a horse, but this I doubt. Bill's cocks always seemed to win, and I felt he got a useful out cross from the Durham miners, who then all had fighting cocks. I know many reading this chapter will be shocked that cockfighting was still going on after the war and will be thinking how cruel etc, etc. For me, were I born a rooster instead of a human, I would rather have been a fighting Old English game cock and been literally 'fed like a fighting cock' (which they were, with a nip of brandy added each day) than been one of those emasculated 'chooks' that are reared in their thousands to be sold in supermarkets! If the fighting cock survived he was given his own harem to breed other champs, in fact he had lived the life of Riley!

But back to those who forwarded the Highland pony breed in England. The Countess Swinton with her well known suffix of 'Dykes' has been a great supporter of the breed, especially in the show ring, and did her stint on Council at the same time as I did thirty-odd years ago. Sadly, because of a hunting accident, she is confined to a wheel chair, but I understand she is a great supporter of all things equine in the House of Lords—and my goodness, we need all the help we can get, as horse supporters are few and far between, especially in the hunting world.

Then of course, as mentioned above, there were the breeders in the South West who formed a group which called itself the South West Peninsula Highland Pony Breeders and were constantly at war with the Highland Pony Society, but what's new? All Breed Societies have radical groups on the one hand and the 'aye beens' (it's aye been done this way), the old and bold who don't want anything changed, on the other. The South West Peninsula were advised and helped, as I say, by Norah Fairfax-Lucy and by Mrs Warren, whose prefix was 'New Calgary', so of course they wanted ponies of what were then known as the 'Western Isles' type. That meant active ponies with quality and riding conformation, that could compete in dressage, cross country, jumping, driving etc. All those disciplines are accepted in Scotland now, but twenty years ago England was far in front. But in those days Mrs Warren was a force to be reckoned with. The power behind the South West Peninsula group was Mrs Mason of the Woodbeer stud. In 1971, when Lady Fairfax-Lucy visited, they had thirty Highland ponies which were competing in dressage, jumping, cross country and ordinary riding classes, way before their time!

Now there are many younger breeders who are keeping the flag flying 'Furth of

Victoria Lloyd riding 'Paramoor Tressa' and winning at the British Nations Cup and Grand Prix, Hickstead, in 1994 (Victoria Lloyd)

Scotland'. Linda Impey has been a great supporter of the breed, not only in the show ring but also on the breed's Council (a costly business for one living in Essex), and she has helped at countless breed functions including their Highland Pony Enthusiasts Club Show every second year at Malvern. Victoria Lloyd, whose photo you see above (and who was one of only two who replied to my plea for Highland pony photos) is typical of the modern person who wishes to get the most out of their Highland pony.

When it comes to Highland cattle in England I have already mentioned Pearson Brown, that superb butcher and showman, and the great job he did for the breed in Yorkshire. Then in Surrey we had my old friend Reg Derisley. Reg was also a butcher and stuck by the breed during those lean years when too many Highland bulls were being produced, when after all they should be a female-producing breed, not a terminal sire breed like the Aberdeen-Angus, Hereford, Charollais or Limousin. Anyway, in the late fifties Reg would be the biggest buyer of Highland bulls at the Oban Sales, and Surrey must have enjoyed some real beef instead of the dairy rubbish they would normally get. The only codicil to that is that if they were unlucky they might have got a piece of some of the old bulls that were sold, because Highland cattle breeders then, knowing that longevity was one of the breed's assets, would often use old, but tried, bulls for breeding and then try to flog them again, so as a result either Reg or the Oban butcher landed up with them. Of one thing I'm sure, they weren't full of BSE because judging by their condition they had been fed mostly on fresh air! It does my old heart good to see Reg's fold at Byfleet in Surrey still going strong in 1996, as he founded it in 1922 and it must be one of the oldest folds in the country that has flown the flag for the Society.

It was Reg and his pal Tom Copas, also from the south, who kept the Highland cattle classes going at Smithfield and JBC. As a Council member and later a Vice-President of the Royal Smithfield Club, and the only one with Highland cattle connections, it was left to me to ensure that a sufficient number of animals from the breed would be entered so that the classes could continue. There was a big increase in Continental breeds wanting classes, and as space in Earls Court is limited, Council decided that unless a breed could produce X number of beasts (I can't remember how many) that breed would be entered with the 'odds and sods' and wouldn't get its own classes. Those breeders who now fill the Highland cattle classes with, may I say, beautifully-presented animals, can thank the late Reg Derisley and Tom Copas for keeping those classes open. And dare I add, as a very dear friend of both, that some of the cattle they showed could have done with a bit of the modern stockman's ability to produce an animal for Smithfield. But they were the forerunners of an explosion of Highland cattle breeders in England.

Tom Copas and his sons bought Remenham Farm at Henley-on-Thames, the fields of which are overlooking the famous Regatta course. I had been lucky enough to be present at a Regatta prior to the Copas takeover, as the previous owner was John Cridlan, a famous Aberdeen-Angus breeder. I remember well John sitting in his office with a bottle of Bell's whisky (of which he took copious drams) on his left side and a huge waste-paper basket on his right side. His general factotum then ushered in the tenants of his river sites, where they had hospitality marquees and where bar owners had taken over a barn or a stable or cattle court as bars for the duration of the Regatta. John, a great friend of mine from Smithfield Show days, was a crusty old character, and as the tenants came in he barked, 'You know your rent, it's XYZ, notes only please and in that basket.' I sat absolutely speechless watching one hundred pound notes, which I had never seen before, and have never had or used, put in this waste-paper basket, and the total sum must have amounted to thousands. However I never got a chance to count them, as I had received my share of the Bell's bottle and I was ushered out with John to see what sort of job his 'tenants' were making of decorating his premises. I remember him telling me that he got his whole steading whitewashed and painted for free by his tenants as part of their (colossal) rent!

But yet again, like Bill Goodson, John and his lovely wife had no family, and the Copas family stepped in. Dear Tom Copas, shortly before he died, invited Sal and myself to one of their hospitality marquees during the Regatta, and we realised how business-like the whole thing had become compared with John's lovely days of notes in the waste-paper basket and drinks in a white-washed byre! Like ever so many sporting events Henley Regatta has gone up-market, and leasing hospitality marquees is now big business. Tom's sons have cottoned on to this, and have done it really well. For the first (and possibly last) time in my life I enjoyed all the fantastic pleasure of not lifting a finger for one whole day (although I lifted my right arm for most of it!) as one was directed to a special car park, taken to the marquee in a Land Rover, waited on hand and foot, and then taken to a launch that cruised up the centre of the Thames to watch whichever event one wanted to see. Actually I enjoyed the jazz band which was on our launch more than the rowing! But I realised during that one day that there is an awful lot of money in that south eastern belt that we never see in Scotland.

For all that, Tom Copas, who had made money out of cherries and other fruits, and also turkeys, in the days before turkey rustlers were two a penny, and brought up his extremely able boys who realised the fantastic potential of the Henley Regatta, for all that, as I say, Tom remained faithful to his Highland cattle. He was still looking after his Smithfield Show entries long after he should have packed it in. The breed owe a lot to Pearson Brown, Reg Derisley and Tom Copas for keeping the breed flag flying during some very dicey years. Sadly none of them got any of the really high prices that were paid by overseas breeders before the advent of BSE, although being near Heathrow Tom did get a few beasts exported.

The new breeders in England are so numerous that I would be unwise to mention some and then antagonise others. However I'm delighted that Judith Dawes is to be (or may already be, depending when this book is published) our President. Firstly, she is no hobby Highland cattle breeder, she is a practical farmer. Secondly, she comes from the south where people have often in the past said they weren't being represented, and often with reason. Thirdly, she is a stockswoman who knows how to show a beast, as I've been honoured to judge a bull she showed at the Three Counties Show in the Supreme Beef Overall Championship which she had produced so well that I so nearly made it the overall Beef Champion. Fourthly, she follows those other lovely ladies who have provided such a backbone to the Highland Cattle Society, and who seem to me, a mere (ancient) male, to have the ability, and perhaps the willingness, to devote more of the time that is needed to make a good job of being President.

With the advent of BSE we have seen a new demand for beef from herds or folds that are naturally reared and fed, and it may well be we will see more owners in England giving serious thought to producing good, tasty, beef from their folds instead

Dr Geoff Sparrow, the 'Hunting Doctor', out with the Southdown Hounds and mounted on 'Greylag of Onyx' (Penny Smith, Nashend)

of having one or two nice looking 'beasties' that give the owners a higher social rating in their area.

Pony-wise in England I am sad to find out only now, in 1996 when I am writing this, that the medical officer of the Sussex Yeomanry who passed me fit for service, all those fifty-nine years ago, was a Highland pony addict. Dr Geoffrey Sparrow, MC, TD, FRCS, whose photo hunting with the Southdown on a Highland pony you see on these pages, was a character if ever there was one. When I met him first he was already famous in Sussex as the 'Hunting Doctor', as opposed to the 'Hunting Parson' which pre-war a friend of my father's said I should be. Geoffrey had served with distinction in World War I in Palestine, Syria etc and won his MC. When I met him in the thirties he was passing recruits like me to serve in the Second World War. He passed me (with one terrible flat foot) because he knew I had played rugby for Horsham some days before my inspection! He was hauled over the coals by a senior officer (but very junior in age), for passing seventy recruits in one night just prior to the outbreak of the war. His reply was, 'If I hadn't passed them, where would we have got the men to fill the Territorial Regiments who helped us win the war?'

I always remember him fondly, as he found out I was keen on sporting things and he took me out to dig badgers with him. He never killed them, he put them in bags and exported them to the West Country, as he reckoned they were more at home there than in the light land of Sussex. He was hunting-daft, and when with us in Hove at the outbreak of war he always wore his breeches and riding boots preparatory to a day's hunting. His two Jack Russell terriers occupied the bed which should have been for patients, of which there were all too many. I was then a Sergeant Major, and had to bring in our latest draft into his surgery. These were Cockneys who had never had a 'jab' in their lives, and one after another they keeled over after they got their TAB innoculation, administered (according to Townsend, Geoffrey's super batman) with needles that had been sharpened on the wall! All the while Geoffrey was telling me all about the super hunt they had had with the Southdown, quite oblivious of the bodies lying around!

While with our regiment at Hove, thanks to his pony-daft wife, Margaret, and his ex-hunt servant batman Townsend, Geoffrey hunted at least three days a week. Luckily the Colonel pre-war had hunted in Ireland, so Geoffrey was lucky, but I doubt there would be a few colonels of regiments who would have put a stop to this great character's exploits. Sadly, because of his age he was taken from us to go to a base job in Palestine and the Egypt, where he hunted foxes yet again. Although all the locals said there were no foxes he was convinced there were. Those of you who, like me, have had the pleasure of seeing that most productive piece of land in the world, i.e. the Nile Delta, will realise that it doesn't look like hunting country, with its deep ditches which irrigate crops of lucerne, barley, cotton, rice, melons, tomatoes, you name it. Its fertility is due to the fantastic soil from the silt brought down by that wonderful river the Nile, which still irrigates it to this day after thousands of years of cultivation. But with regard to the foxes Geoffrey was, as always, right, as with his two Salukis that he had trained to hunt, he accounted for seven and a half brace of foxes, two brace of mongoose and five wild cats, much to the joy of the fellaheen (the local smallholders), as they had been told by their feudal landlords that the poultry which were disappearing were taken by two-legged, not four-legged vermin! I don't know what conditions are like in Egypt today, but people in this country who moaned about the feudal system in Britain pre-war should have seen what was going on out there sixty years ago!

Sadly, after the war, finding a job, keeping it, having a family, educating them, making a living etc, etc. left me little time to keep in touch with my Sussex Yeomanry mates. When I went back to Sussex it was to the Queen Victoria Hospital in East Grinstead to have a further operation or check-up from the great Sir Archie McIndoe, and after each visit I had to rush back to my job. The result is that until Penny Smith of Nashend lent me Geoff Sparrow's book this year, I never knew that

Shirley MacGregor, one of the pioneers of driving Highland ponies, driving a pair in tandem: not the easiest combination to drive, but used in the old days when the lead horse was needed for fox-hunting. What easier way to get him to the meet, with saddle, food and drink in the trap, and a second horse if required 'waiting in the wings' (Shirley MacGregor)

Geoff rode Highland ponies to hunt with the Southdown (and with Jimmy Edwards, the comedian with the huge moustache), or that Margaret Sparrow, who showed Highland ponies each year at the Royal Highland, was his widow. Now there was a character if ever there was one. At the Royal Highland they supply you with as much green feed (usually long forced grass, as the date is late June) as you can carry. Margaret, who was extremely small in stature, worked out that if she carried the grass in a normal sheet (not one for sleeping on but a hessian sack ripped up to form a square) then she wouldn't be able to carry much, so having been brought up in the East where women carry enormous loads on their heads, or attached to their fore-heads and actually carried on their backs, she had a special sheet made that was the envy of all the other Highland pony breeders, who watched in amazement as this wee woman went off with a sheetful that looked bigger than she was!

I suppose the quieter tempo of life bred more characters in the past, or was it the fact there was no TV, or is it just an old man's imagination? I think they are getting fewer. Having said that I remember well standing beside the late 'Shimi', Lord Lovat, in 1954 at a Beef Shorthorn dinner drinks party in Perth before the annual

Bull Sales. He was, as always, looking every inch the clan chieftain, with that wonderful slightly arrogant but immensely handsome face, dressed in his Fraser kilt and his patched tartan stockings and with a large glass of whisky in his hand, but through and through a leader of men and an outstanding Highlander. He turned to me, as I was MC that night, and said, 'Ben, couldn't you have got some of the characters here tonight or are they all dead?' To which I replied, 'Sir, I'm not a thousand miles from one right now.'

I know there are so many dedicated Highland pony and cattle breeders south of the border that I should have mentioned and haven't, but as one gets older one doesn't move around as much as one used to do, and as I said in the Acknowledgements it's impossible to name everyone. However, of one thing I am certain, that the input the English have put into both breeds has been immense, and sadly has not been appreciated to the extent it should have been, especially in the Highland Pony Society. As for the Highland Cattle Society, more of their breeders had English connections, which meant their outlook was broader than the old 'Here's tae us wha's like us.' Nuff said before I get shot by some well known Scottish Highland pony breeders!

13
Highland Ponies and Cattle Overseas

Before the present great demand for our ponies from Europe I have no evidence of earlier exports, apart from the one from Calgary and the other from Nashend already mentioned. There must have been the odd one here and there, but the one that I had more than a little to do with myself was the one that was exported to the famous King Ranch in Texas in 1960.

Why I call the King Ranch famous is because it is where the owner, Bob Kleberg, bred the well-known 'Santa Gertrudis' breed of cattle out of three-eighths Beef Shorthorn and five-eighths Brahman. The contribution of the Beef Shorthorn was to put flesh on the Brahman, which, with its hump, like a camel, can withstand the terrific heat in its native India, and as a result has been used in hot spots all over the world, like Texas and parts of Australia. Bob, having got more flesh on the breed, with the aid of a very able scientist, whose name I think was Armstrong, 'fixed the type' as we say in the stock breeding world. This meant that, instead of getting a certain number of the progeny as Shorthorn and the others Brahman when you crossed the two breeds, they came out consistently with the characteristics of both as Bob wanted them to.

As I had seen the Cadzow brothers form the 'Luing' breed of cattle in Scotland from cross-Highland heifer calves, most of which were bought from Glenlochay while I was the manager there, I was desperately keen to visit the King Ranch about which I had heard and read so much. Talk about good luck, I've had it all my life: just then in 1959 I was chosen to go on a Ford Foundation/Nuffield scholarship to study beef production in the U.S.A. Of course at that time the mass feeding of cattle, like barley beef, was coming into vogue in this country, so I had to go to the places where this was being done in the States. I was not impressed with their massive feed lots. Luckily, however, the girl in charge of deciding where we were to go on our tour was both a keen and a super dancer, and all those years ago I could do a nifty soft-shoe shuffle! Result, I was booked into the King Ranch for a visit.

When I got there, and it's on the Mexican border, the temperature was one hundred degrees plus, but the cottage I was shown into by John Cypher, the P.R.O., was delightfully cool, and believe it or not had a bottle of whisky and a jug of iced water placed by my bed! John apologised profusely for the non-appearance of the Klebergs, as the King Ranch Annual Sale of bulls had been held the previous week and they were whacked. He said he would show me round etc. etc, and would be back to take me out for a meal later that evening.

I always wore my kilt on these overseas trips, as I found it the best possible passport, but when the temperature is in the hundreds it's very hot and sweaty. As I'd come quite a bit of the journey by train, and that meant a distance of hundreds of miles, I decided to get a bit of exercise, which is sometimes hard to take on these kind of trips. So I set off up the road beside the cottage and was confronted by a huge Cadillac which came to a standstill beside me. A very handsome middle-aged lady asked in an American accent what my 'plaid' was (the Americans always call tartan 'plaid'). She then asked what I was doing there dressed in a kilt, etc. etc. and drove off. When I got back to the cottage all hell had been let loose, my bag had been moved up to the big 'hoose' and the poor P.R.O. had been given a dressing-down because (a) he hadn't told the Klebergs I was a Scot (the lady in the Cadillac was none other than Mrs Kleberg, and she was a Campbell descended from the Argylls) and (b) I wasn't just rubber-necking and knew a wee bit about cattle.

The next few days were some of the most memorable in my extraordinarily diverse but very happy life. Bob was having his portrait painted by Simon Elwes, the well-known English portrait painter who was also staying at the ranch, but the two did not get on at all. Bob would never sit still for long and was always asking, 'When can I go and ride?' Elwes was having marital problems, and until we'd all had one or two 'libations' round the swimming pool before the evening meal, things were, to say the least, very touchy. But during the day Bob was absolutely marvellous. I will never forget the time he spent showing me his cattle and his Quarter horses (so-called because they are the fastest breed over a quarter-mile, which is all you need them to do to cut out the cattle), and the fantastic job he had done clearing thousands of acres of 'Mesquite', a weed like gorse, and just as prickly, as I was to find out when I backed into a bush wearing my kilt! And then the day when we were both mounted on Quarter horses, and his horse reared as it saw a snake rise in front of it, and Bob pulled his revolver out of its holster and shot it through the head! Then we had a day shooting, I think quail, or was it sand-grouse? I asked him, 'have you ever shot driven grouse?' As the answer was in the negative I was ordered to organize a driven grouse day in Scotland for the Klebergs in 1960. By that time I was managing for Michael Noble, Secretary of State for Scotland, who was delighted to organise some shooting for Bob. Sadly I didn't see Bob and his wife Helen again after this, but the one thing I was able to do was to see that Michael took him to a grouse moor that used Highland ponies. He, great horseman that he was, ordered one to be sent out to the King Ranch. As this all happened thirty-six years ago, there is now no-one left over in Texas whom I knew then, so I don't know what happened to the pony.

Since those early days the King Ranch has expanded into Australia, South Africa and many other countries, and has diversified into, among other things, thoroughbred racehorses. When Sal and I were in Kentucky a few years ago and attended a Thoroughbred Yearling Sale the King Ranch had quite a few entries, and the grooms were turned out immaculately with 'King Ranch' emblazoned on their green sweaters—all very smart and just as Bob, that super old showman, would have wanted it.

In the Department of Agriculture Stud Book records there is an entry in 1954 of a mouse dun stallion, 'Ben Challum' being sold to Israel for one hundred pounds. Before going out he had served six mares in the previous covering season, after being placed second at the Royal Highland Show at Alloa that year.

Before the Royal Highland Show eventually came to rest permanently at Ingliston it toured the country, and at each place it visited has left memories with me that I'll have all my life, whereas sadly the ones at Ingliston have taken on, for me at least, a sameness. The Glasgow one, pre-war, reminds me of the scene I depicted in an earlier chapter with the wee Glasgow keelie, nicely drunk, trying to get onto a Highland pony stallion's back. Melrose, also before the war, is memorable for its wonderful show of Border sheep brought out to perfection by (to my mind) the world's greatest shepherds. Inverness immediately after the war was notable for its fantastic traffic jams, as all the Highland 'bobbies' went off for their tea at the same time; and for me there was the thrill of staying at Beaufort Castle and being treated as an equal by my wartime hero and later friend, 'Shimi', the Lord Lovat. The Dundee Show was smothered in an ever-present blanket of dust, as the show was held on the district rubbish coup! The combination of the dust and the heat—yes, it was a very hot show too—added considerably to the thirsts of the cattlemen for whom I was responsible, and left me without a ha'penny! Aberdeen was the wettest show ever, but because of it one of the happiest. Waitresses lost their shoes in the mud, wellington boots and umbrellas were sold out on the first day, and the carpet in the huge Entrance Hall of the Station Hotel had to be renewed at vast cost because they couldn't remove the mud that got on it! But everyone smiled, and I got to know the late Dr 'Jimmy' Durno, who was President that year, and although he was soaking wet he visited every, yes, every, stand and breed section. What a gentleman, and I'm proud to have known him.

But the Alloa Show, where 'Ben Challum', the D.O.A.S stallion, came second, I remember for a rather distressing reason. When I was tenant at Gaskbeg in Upper Speyside I had a spare cottage, as this was in the days before these sort of cottages were sought after by townees longing to see how we country folk lived, and from time to time I used it to take in a student. Brother Frank, by that time a Brigadier in the Regular Army, recommended to me a certain Major who wanted to 'become a farmer' on his Army retirement. As he had no farming background whatsoever and was desperately keen to know where he could get some rough shooting I should have smelt a rat! But who was I, who had left the Army as a wounded Captain, to argue with my wee brother when he said, 'He seems a good sort of chap'. When the said chap turned up he had three Jack Russell terriers, which turned out to be the be all and end all of his life! Although Army trained he was never 'on parade' in time because those bloody wee dogs hadn't been run, or one hadn't finished its breakfast or another hadn't done its 'jobbie' or something. He made a middling attempt at work in what I always call the 'spring rush' of the lambing and the cultivations to do with the sowing of the spring crops—at one thousand feet above sea level you don't get many days to do them. Anyway, after having not done too much to help with the spring work on the farm the gallant Major announced he had to get off to go to the Highland Show, as he had to meet a great friend who also bred Jack Russells and discuss a mating with one of the Major's bitches. This was always a busy time for us on hill farms, because we all 'neighboured' to castrate our ram lambs and to clip our ewe hoggs, and there were five 'neighbours' around so one was bound to be working Highland Show week. Despite this I softly said he could go, mainly because I thought he would be useless on a big clipping day!

The Show at Alloa was one of the hottest I can remember, and I was there for a couple of days, stewarding as far as I can remember. The gallant Major, who always told me off for having my working collies kennelled up except when I wanted to work them or exercise them had, believe it or not, taken his three terriers with him to the Show in his wee van with a tin roof (as they all had just after the war), had locked it up and came back at the end of the day to find three corpses. Yes, I remember the Alloa Show all too vividly, it was blazing hot, and so was my temper with that idiot who (like all too many R.S.P.C.A. supporters) didn't understand basic animal husbandry. Nowadays the police go round the car parks, and if they find a dog or dogs under stress in a locked-up car, if the owner doesn't come immediately in response to a tannoy announcement, they break a hole in one of the door windows.

I seem to have strayed a long way from my theme of Highland ponies and cattle, but all the Highland Shows I have attended since my first in 1929 have been part of my experience of the breeds. Ben Coutts has been cattleman, owner, steward, judge, commentator, groom in the Highland Pony Driving Class, Breed President, or just one of the thousands who, in the palmy post-war days when Scotland was full of the world's best stocksmen, went to the Highland Show to meet fellow stocksmen.

Apart from the odd export of ponies further afield that I have mentioned, most recent exports have been to Europe which, considering its size, has few pony breeds compared with Britain. When you think of it, in our comparatively wee country we have the Highlands, Shetlands, Dales, Fells, Welsh Cobs, Welsh ponies, New Forest, Dartmoor, Exmoor, along with the Connemara ponies from Ireland, and all with some attribute to give to the equine world in Europe. The Highland has suited many because of its ability to outwinter and live on paltry rations compared with a thoroughbred type, handy to be caught up at the weekend to be ridden, and above all because of its docile temperament—too much so as far as some of the young are concerned. However I know from bitter experience that it is Dad and Mum in this country, and 'Papa' and 'Maman' in France who have to do the twice-a-day mucking out of that 'whizzy' pony that has to be in-wintered!

The French were in the vanguard of those in Europe who realised the potential of the Highland pony breed. One customer was a nature reserve, where they wanted ponies to run wild over their vast expanses of land, and instead of using the white horses of the Camargue they chose Highland ponies. There was Madame Buchaillat,

Anne Buchaillat's team of eight matched Highland ponies, driven by her son Patrice
(Madame Anne Buchaillat)

whose wonderful team of eight driven Highland ponies you can see above. The French have that flair for putting on displays that we Scots lack. Is it the lack of sunshine, wine, or our native dourness?—but Madame's open Highland Pony Days put us to shame. She has a Cossack display, horseball, mounted archery and her son's magnificent driving turnouts: not only the one shown, but also teams of four, tandems and teams of three etc. etc.: in fact, Madame, you put us Scots to shame when it comes to promoting the breed.

Thanks are due to Christine Northcott, who transferred her affections from Devon to Brittany, but luckily for the breed took her love of Highland ponies with her. She indoctrinated Christian Michielini, chairman of Brittany Ferries, who has kindly sponsored the Breed Shows, giving the prize of a free week's holiday to the winners of the in-hand, ridden and driven classes at the show. Sal won this prize with her driven mare 'Lochlands Galliard', and so off we set on a Brittany Ferry to Roskoff, to be met by Christine and Christian. They showed us just how far behind we, who bred the Highland ponies initially, are in the international world of horse breeding today. They showed us their stallion, 'Inverquarity Playboy', being jumped over poles without a rider on board and obviously enjoying the performance hugely. All the stallions in France and Germany have to pass some sort of performance test before they get a licence. How I wish that we, as the 'oldie of all oldies' in the breed, did the same sort of thing: if we don't, we will end up, as in all too many other things, being controlled by other European countries. The two 'Christians' took us to a super horse fair, where we saw cossack riding, shoeing demonstrations and all sorts of horse-related sports, which the French townees lapped up, as would our townees. All too often our Agricultural Shows have become hidebound, and instead of making the afternoon's entertainment orientated to the country they pander to what they *think* the townees want. Mind you, the weather in France, the wine and the French love of their food fairly helps their summer events. Their barbecues of real meat, not beefburgers, washed down with the local vino, did a lot to convince me that that wee local show was one of the best I've seen.

Then Germany came on the scene, as strongly as they did with their demand for Highland cattle. It's always sad to my mind that certain breeders, in all breeds, try to corner a market and say 'this territory is mine'. When the German market started to open up Herr Philipp was very open about the fact that he wasn't going to be linked to any one member or section of the Highland Pony Society and would deal with anyone. I pull his leg about his taste (or lack of it) when dressing up as a 'Highland Chentleman', but I admire his stand against the big guns in the Society who would like to take over the very considerable German market. It is a rich country with an expanding town population but with an essentially rural background, so what happens? The genes exert themselves, and all the daughters want a pony. However they are studying or working all week, so they buy a Highland pony, leave it out all week and bring it up and ride it at the weekend.

There are many in Germany who have promoted the breed, like Christine Decker, but Erika and Ernst Baumer have been tremendous supporters not only of our ponies but of our Highland cattle. Ernst, who is the first to admit he made a fortune from realising how essential mobile phones were to be in this technological age, as far as I can gather bought up all the rights to all the mobile phones in Germany, and then sold them at the right time. (If I'm wrong about this, I know either Ernst or Erika, both good friends, will tell me off in the nicest way!) What I do know to be true is that they decided to use the fairly considerable amount of money they made, or at least some of it, on breeding, finishing and killing their own cattle, and selling them in their own butcher's shops. To begin with they imported Highlands, Galloways and Shorthorns, mainly from Scotland, and then B.S.E. struck. I know how easy it is to criticise the Government, but their handling of the B.S.E. problem in March 1996 was a complete disaster.

But meantime, just before the B.S.E. crisis, the Baumers started to build up a very substantial stud of Highland ponies. Among other ponies they have imported 'Falcron Frost', who had done everything possible in Scotland, having won the in-hand and ridden championships at the R.H.A.S., plus too many other championships to mention, and 'Lochlands Galliard', which as described earlier had just won the Mountain and Moorland Scottish Driving Championship, when owned and driven by my wife Sal. Scott MacGregor had produced the former and Sally the latter. The Baumers did me the honour of asking me to judge their pre-sale show of Highland and Galloway cattle, and I only wish some shows in this country were as generous in their expenses as were the Baumers. Sadly there is now a strong anti-British cattle feeling in Germany, and I'm told that even descendants of British cattle are being slaughtered 'just for fear' they carry the dreaded B.S.E.

One of the greatest supporters of Highland cattle among European countries is Austria. A certain Arnold Forstein came to the bull sales in Oban in 1988 and luckily met Angus MacKay, ex-Society President and a good talker (and an even better singer). Arnold had no English, nor had Angus any German, but the outcome of their meeting was highly successful, as Forstein went back with a Balmoral bull that had been Champion, and which went on to sire a lot of good cattle that now find their way into the top fashionable restaurants in Vienna. Angus went out to Austria to follow up his initial meeting with Arnold, and was amazed to find nearly one hundred folds of Highlanders there!

The thing that impresses me about the Austrians' wish to import Highland cattle is the fact that they want to use them for the job for which our forefathers bred them, i.e. to graze the roughage on the high hills in summer, while winter keep was made in the straths and glens for the long winter months. Arnold had found out that since the old system of putting cows out to the hills in summer had been discontinued there were more avalanches. This was because instead of the cattle leaving a bare sward, there was long grass at the start of winter. When the winter snow started to melt it caught on the long grass and took it with it, as well as the all-important top soil. Well, it seems the Highlanders, if they were not being used for exactly the same job they were bred for in Scotland, taking off the Molinia and Nardus grasses to let the sheep get a sweet bite of the shorter herbage, were at least being put to the right sort of use by the Austrians. I hear the Balmoral bull is still working and leaving super stock. We occasionally get worrying reports in this country about the Monarchy and the succession, but the Queen's bull in Austria is certainly guaranteeing the succession of Highland cattle over there, and making sure there are going to be good steaks in Vienna.

Following on the export of Highland bulls that Tommy MacDonald and I organised all those years ago, I was more than pleased to hear from Angus about the outstanding fold he had seen on a visit to the States. It was owned by a Jack Strow, and comprised eight hundred head! And he had got his bulls from my old friend Baxter Berry, who had some of those bulls we had exported all those forty-plus years ago. Jack Strow, like the Austrians, was using his Highland cattle as they were meant to be used. His ranch was five thousand feet above sea level. He made them work for their feed, and only gave them a feed block that had a twenty-five per cent protein content. The rest they had to find for themselves, and at five thousand feet there isn't much to find!

I was very pleased to hear that a Glenfinglas bull, bred by the late Jack Cameron, which I had made Champion at the Oban Bull Sales (when it was led round the ring by one John B. Cameron, then a wee laddie and now one of our few farming millionaires), had bred extremely well over in the States.

All the units in the States, whatever breed they use, try to have somewhere to

Highland cattle at Maple Lea Farm, Canada, seen in their natural surroundings
(Highland Cattle Society)

finish their cattle. Denver has always been the top spot for finished cattle, and I'm proud to say that I've been to those fantastic stockyards.

Canada also has a burgeoning Highland cattle business. There was a Douneside bull that was bought at two thousand, four hundred guineas (which we all thought a lot of money at the time) by a Mr Osprey of Canada, and he has gone on to do a great job. Judy Bowser, that great breed supporter and friend of mine, will be sorry that she sold 'Gillie Buidh of Ben More' privately to a Canadian buyer, as I hear he has bred some super big, fleshy cattle, but what a good advert for the breed! Canadian breeders were able to take advantage of the B.S.E. crisis, in that they were able to export their cattle, when we were no longer able to, to Denmark where there is a thriving Society. Perhaps as in the U.K. there may be all too many Danish breeders whose main aim is to have nice-looking cattle on their small patch of land, but who knows, some Danish townees may find that beef from Highland cattle reared traditionally tastes that wee bit better than beef from all too many of the feed lots worldwide that have done meat-eating so much harm.

Holland I have always thought of as a flat arable country, specialising in bulbs and vegetables, but I didn't know they had an area near the German border where there is woodland and where they wanted cattle to keep the herbage in trim, in the same way as we have done in the Highlands and as the Austrians are doing. Someone from

Holland who must have known about cattle came to Scotland and decided to buy some cows at the Douglas and Angus reduction sale. Why I say this person must have known about cattle is firstly, because in my humble opinion it was the top fold in the country, not one that went for prize tickets at the shows or bull sales, but one that had consistently bred good honest cattle with bone and substance, right on their legs, with good feet, nicely fleshed and with character written all over their faces, which always denotes a good beast. Secondly, because he bought the lean cows that were the ones that made the least money—but why were they lean? Because they had been working at bringing up a big calf. It always amazes me how many people buy an over-fat beast. If she is a cow or mare she hasn't been doing her job right, and if he is a bull or stallion he may not be able to do his job right!

The result of the Dutchman's wise purchases was an influx of some Strathallan blood (which pleases me, as I was instrumental in buying some of their foundation stock in the late forties) into the Dutch fold, which is now looked upon as being one of the best in Europe. They were bought to do the specific job of controlling the herbage in a conservation area, but because those responsible have started to look on the whole project as a commercial one they have taken their steers through to the finishing stage and developed a niche market for their meat in a top-class chain of restaurants, so that now they have turned them into a commercially viable herd.

Could there be a lesson here for us in the U.K.? This, I am delighted to say, is an issue now being attended to by the Highland Cattle Society, with the establishing of Highland Beef Ltd. This approach will be badly needed in the future. As fewer people eat beef because of scares like B.S.E. and the E. Coli outbreak, those that do eat it will demand the best quality and will want it to be naturally reared as well— what better to supply this requirement than Highland beef?

One wouldn't naturally think of Australia's climate as being conducive to Highland cattle. Their coats are like having a Macintosh (the long outer hair for shedding the rain) worn over a woolly waistcoat to keep them warm. But Australia, with its vastness, can have all sorts of weather within it. Sal and I nearly froze one night when we visited a Scottish widower and he put us in his spare room which was a tin bothy. The beds hadn't been slept in or aired for goodness knows how long, there was a keen frost outside and we never slept a wink. Highland cattle would have done well on that station, wherever else they breed them on that vast continent. But in fact they have a thriving Society, and in the Scottish Society's newsletter of December 1966 there is a photo of their Supreme Champion at their indoor winter show, and she looks a good heifer to me.

There are Highland ponies in Australia too, and I had the pleasure of taking two of the breed's greatest Australian supporters up to my old stamping ground, Glenartney, on a magical late September morning. There they saw four white deer ponies tacked up with their deer saddles ready for the hill, and the stalkers dressed in plus four suits made up in the Estate tweed of purplish colour (to make them as inconspicuous as possible against the heather). There's no doubt it made the Aussies' trip, as on the drive home to Woodburn they bombarded me with questions about the deer saddles, and why did the stalkers carry those neatly coiled-up ropes (the ones for dragging the stag to the pony) etc. etc.

So all in all, there is a worldwide demand for our Highland ponies and cattle, as there always has been for our Highland folk. Now let's have a 'Coutts' eye view' of what he thinks the future holds for all three breeds!

14

The Future of the Three Breeds as the Author Sees It

How I'd love to see Highland ponies back on the crofts and small farms, instead of those rusting old Fergie tractors that cost a fortune to replace. How I would love to see all deer forests, like Balmoral, using Highland ponies instead of the vehicles now used in the majority of them. How I would love to see Highland ponies in their traps being used to take the farmer and his wife to market, instead of those smelly, all too fast, cars we now use. But one can't turn back the clock and one must be realistic. Anyway, who am I to talk about using a pony and trap as a means of transport, as just after the war I was more than happy to join the car-owners! I was engaged to manage one thousand acres of arable land with thirty-three employees (including a butler, a cook, housemaids, gardeners, gamekeeper, estate workers etc.), a pedigree Shorthorn herd, plus two other estates, one of which had a pedigree Highland cattle fold on it and the third with six thousand Blackface breeding ewes, and all the labour required to keep the estates going. My wage was six pounds per week, but I got an estate van instead of a pony and trap so that I could move around quicker, and I loved it!

So where can we see the future for the Highland pony breed? The division between the so-called 'Western Isles type' and the 'Garron type' has gone, and most people want free-moving ponies which retain the breed's ability to be out-wintered at low cost and yet be got up at the weekend to be ridden. There has been a tremendous improvement in breeding ponies with performance potential, like Audrey Barron's 'Kincardine Ben MacDhui', which at the time of writing is at the elementary level in dressage competitions. Even a few years ago few would ever have believed it possible for a Highland pony to do a dressage test, never mind get to that level. In ridden classes 'Acorn of Kinnoull', owned by R. and L. Fraser and and ridden by Jane McNaught represented the breed right royally at Olympia in finishing up third overall in the ridden Mountain and Moorland Championship.

In the driving scene we are seeing the same thing, people are realising their potential. Of course there are slugs, as there are slugs in thoroughbreds. You just want to talk to a jockey and he'll tell you. As one well-known Northern-based jockey told me about a horse I had a very small share in when he was unsaddling him, 'Get rid of him quick, boss, he's a slug.' But the Highland pony breed has a lot to offer in this day and age of affluence. Oh, I know there will be readers who think

The 'sCoutts Greys'—the author and family mounted on Highland and cross-Highland ponies

they are not affluent compared with the people they see on T.V., but compared with the days when I was first connected with the breed we are an affluent society, and the Highland pony breeders are benefiting. In 1996 I heard of a Highland pony breeder in England who sold a filly foal (six months old) for one thousand pounds to someone who wanted a pet! But this is a one-off, and the majority of ponies get broken—though 'there's the rub', as Will Shakespeare said, because there are all too few people who can make and break ponies. Thank goodness, however, these folk, thanks to Pony Clubs and Riding Clubs, are becoming more numerous, and the number of ridden Highland ponies at all our shows has risen dramatically. Also, many more ponies are being broken to harness specially for private driving. Leslie MacRonald in Aberdeenshire, although he doesn't drive Highland ponies in his own famous tandem, has broken many Highland ponies for owners at a very reasonable price.

I must say I always remember as a laddie staying with a farmer in Norfolk where I was working for my keep, and although I was a relation the only times I was accepted as family was when I sang in the choir, as I had a half-decent voice, and also when I drove his pony and trap to market five miles distant. What a lovely way to see 'England's green and pleasant land', and Scotland's too, if only there were fewer cars on the road.

The Highland Pony Society have rightly called theirs 'The Versatile Breed', and there is no doubt that the way forward will be in the riding, driving, dressage etc. events rather than in use as croft ponies, grouse-pannier ponies, deer-stalking ponies or even as ponies to be used in the extraction of the vast amount of sitka spruce that will be due to be felled in the next few years. I sincerely hope that ponies will be needed for the latter category of jobs, which after all they were bred to do, but the swing today is to leisure use so the Society must go with the times.

How things have changed over the sixty years I've been associated with the breed. I've been lucky enough to see some of the records kept by the Department of Agriculture's stud at Inverness, and the person responsible for closing that down deserves to be shot (if not hung, drawn and quartered!) As described earlier, that stud, thanks to Jimmie Dean and his minions, had concentrated the best bloodlines in the country, to which any breeder could take a mare and for a very small fee have her served by the top stallions to be found anywhere. As I write I'm looking at 'Glenmuick's' (born 1959) show record. He won just about every championship he could, and was invited to the Ponies of Britain Peterborough Show, where he qualified to be exhibited at the Horse of the Year Show at Wembley, having beaten the thoroughbred! He was always my pin-up, and died at the stud aged eighteen, having done a wonderful job for the breed. The Department always named their stallions 'Ben' or 'Glen'. One I feel sorry for was 'Glenprosen', who was sent to Bernera in 1944 and died swimming ashore. Nature gets rid of the ones it thinks are not fit to breed! Nowadays every human and animal must be allowed to live, but back in

My pin-up Highland pony, 'Glenmuick' (D.O.A.S. Dispersal Sale Catalogue 1977)

those days it was the survival of the fittest—ponies like 'Bain's Horse' that I talked about in a previous chapter: what a grand job he did!

It was in 1923 that a meeting was held in the 'Caley' (Caledonian) Hotel in Edinburgh to form the Highland Pony Society, as an affiliate of the National Pony Society, with as its President J. Munro Mackenzie O.B.E. of Calgary, Mull. The list of Honorary Presidents reads like a Who's Who of Scottish Highland Lairds: the Marquis of Graham, Brodick (about to be the Duke of Montrose); the Earl of Ancaster, owner of the Glenartney stud; Lord Glentanar, Aberdeenshire, whose son I was to help with his Highland Cattle fold in the fifties; the Earl of Leven and Melville from Glenferness; Sir John Stirling Maxwell of Pollock, whose wonderful collection of art treasures is now housed in that great Pollock Museum in Glasgow, which is such a must-see for everyone, even the author, who is not too well versed in things arty and crafty! Then the working committee was composed of the factors and managers of many of the well known Scottish estates: Bob Inglis, factor of the Blair Atholl Estate; John Ferguson, Manager of Glenartney; Donald MacKelvie, a tenant of the Montrose Estates; and James Mackillop, Factor on Islay—all of whom I met as a laddie! There are also many more of whom I have no knowledge, making a vast, and I would have thought unworkable, committee of twenty-three! I have found that the best size of a committee is five, as the chair can hold the balance and you don't get too much talking. Of course the ideal would be one—but that would smack too much of dictatorship!

Believe it or not the first committee meeting was taken over by an argument about the size of ponies. I have mentioned it before, but there were then two classes at the Highland Show, one for the Western Isles type and one for the then normal garron type. It seems there was a big movement from the Island representatives that their height should be not more than fourteen hands, following which motion a heated discussion took place—so, seventy-four years on, what's new?

What is new is that now the Council minutes are typed, whereas back then they were handwritten in the most lovely copper-plate handwriting. What is not new is the fact that some Societies expect so much from a secretary for a meagre salary. There was an argument back in the Highland Pony Society's early meetings as to whether they ought to pay the secretary his expenses, as he was already getting fifteen pounds per annum. Big deal!

These old Council meeting minutes make marvellous reading to one who has been a President, Council member, Chief Executive/Secretary and Judge of different breed societies, as seventy-three years on, little, except the way money has been devalued, has changed! All breed societies have their 'Aye Beens'—'It's aye been done this way'—and they won't budge. I suppose it was those horrific times in the twenties and early thirties, when farming was really up against it, that made all too many farmers careful of every penny: these farmers became, when on a breed society committee, not just canny but really mean. Back in 1924 the Highland Pony Society made the healthy profit of forty-one pounds and eighteen shillings! Some of the committee members who had other interests outside farming, like 'Gillie' MacBeth of Dunira, Comrie, (whom I worked for as a boy) who had ship-building money, and Donald MacKelvie of Lamlash with his grocery business and his famous country-wide potato business, voted that five pounds should be offered to breeders who would go to show examples of the breed at the great Horse Show at Wembley. What happened? The 'Aye Beens' got up and said that Highland ponies were a Scottish breed and should remain so. How petty can you be? But here we are, seventy-odd years on, with a Society that has tremendous potential in England and overseas, and we still have people getting up at the Annual General Meeting saying they don't agree with a rise in this or that certificate, this or that membership, or with anything that would give the Society the money they need to publicise the breed.

As I say, the position of being a breed Society Secretary has not improved, and all too many breed Societies have undervalued and underpaid their Secretaries. My old Dad, a Church of Scotland minister, told me: 'If you work for a committee never do more than nine years. The first three they idolise you, the next three they criticise you and the last three they scandalise you, that's when to get out.' I followed his advice to the day when I was Secretary of the Aberdeen-Angus Society. But what saddens me is that Council members of breed Societies don't go into their Society offices and see the work that running a modern Society entails. The Highland Pony Society are looking for a new Secretary as I write, but if they want to be recognised as one of the leading pony breeds in Britain they must pay him or her (and there are more females who know about ponies than there are males today) the right salary and expenses, and back them to the hilt. I know, having done the job, one has one's faults, and there is no way the Highland Pony Society will get the Angel Gabriel, but I predict a great future for the breed if the Council put the breed's interests first and not their own selfish ends.

The future of the Highland Cattle Society has been tainted by the German approach to the B.S.E. crisis. However there has been a fantastic home demand since that crisis, but what saddens me as an 'oldie' is the lack of real stocksmen and women who are coming into the breed. OK, it's lovely to motor through the Highlands and see a Highland cow and calf at a visitor centre, as we have in Crieff, or some three-year-old bullocks outside every other Highland hotel, but that wasn't the job for which our forefathers bred them. I most sincerely hope that some Government under the influence of someone of standing (but in the absence of the Alec Douglas-Homes, the Michael Nobles and Hector Munros etc., where do we find them?) will realise that we need cattle back on the hills to get rid of that Molinia and Nardus grass that are the curse of good grazing. After all, our forefathers weren't fools: they had to live on what their hills could provide, and Highland cattle were an integral part of this resource.

I see from the latest Highland Cattle Society Newsletter that Highland Beef Limited have got off to a flying start, and I sincerely hope that those who have committed themselves and their money to the scheme will back it wholeheartedly and not send their stock elsewhere for another quid or two. Oh, you may think I'm an old cynic, but I've seen it happen time and again, with even directors of struggling Auction Marts consigning their stock to their competitors. This happened to me when I got Aberdeen and Northern marts to back the Kingussie Mart in the fifties. I as Chairman went round all the local farmers and crofters telling them it was for them I was doing this, since as a personal friend of the Fraser family of MacDonald Fraser and Co., who were giving up the Mart, I would normally have gone instead to their Marts in Perth or Inverness. The reason I was keen to keep Kingussie going was that I had heard so often in clubs and pubs that it was great to save on transport, you could show your stock looking better, it would be especially handy for the autumn sales when one was bringing in the smaller lots etc. etc. So I went ahead, and what happened? We had a wonderful first autumn sale with a super top wether lamb price, I think it was six pounds, for a pen from a farm I managed, Ruthven; a great suckled calf sale and a top cast ewe sale. After that, however, when we had our first middling sale, the locals who had said they would back it melted away like snow off a dyke. I'm delighted to say that despite this, forty years on, the Mart is doing really well. But I only hope that the consignors to Highland Beef Ltd. will stick with them through thick and thin, and believe me, there always is a thin in farming. I've seen a few, but recently, thank God, none as bad as the days when I was a farm worker in the thirties.

I do hope that Highland Beef will remember that Highland cattle are a slow-maturing breed, and that a mature bullock, properly hung, will taste so much better than one that is killed too early. I think it's sad that modern housewives, the few that still cook and don't rely on take-aways and restaurants, don't seem to know that good tasty beef should not be a bright red colour (often looking like that because of the red strip-light over it) but, as I've said before, should be mahogany-coloured. How one educates the young modern housewife about meat completely defeats me. But all power to Highland Beef Ltd., and to Mike Gibson for the great job he has done in advertising the beef from the breed through his 'Macbet'.

But for all these super efforts to sell the steers (as after all fifty per cent of one's calf crop are males, and all too few of these are worth keeping as bulls) Highland cattle are a female-producing breed. In my fifty years of managing and farming hill land I have found cross Highland heifers (Shorthorn cross Highland) to be the ideal hill cow. It annoys me to see Highland and Island farms on T.V. farming programmes featuring Heinz 57 varieties of hill cows. All too often they are cross-continental cows and usually thin-skinned: they were not bred for our wet and cold climate and cannot cope unless they are housed and fed much better than a cross Highland or cross Galloway cow. In the photo overleaf of the Oban Bull Sales of 1953, at which the author showed his Highland bull that was adjudged Reserve Champion (but made the top price of three hundred and twenty guineas—a fortune to me then) you will see a crowded ringside of crofters, farmers et al., all men and women of the land. Forty-four years on we have the biggest entry at the February sales that we've ever seen, but sadly there are few farmers bidding for the animals on offer. Breeding good stock takes a lifetime, and sadly today everyone is in too much of a hurry. This

Oban Bull Sale in the open air at Thomas Corson's Mart, 1953

means few are willing to buy Highland heifers and a Shorthorn bull and wait for four years until they see a decent return on the sale of their three-year-old heifers. I'm convinced however that this is what will be wanted as the Scottish beef herd shrinks and quality will be the name of the game.

The Highland Cattle Society also has its 'Aye Beens' who reckon their Secretary is being paid too much, but as an ex-Secretary I realise what a pile of work he is getting through, and I think he is doing a great job. There is a fantastic explosion of membership, though all too few who are dedicated cattlemen/women. Having said that, it does my heart good to see how many practical stocksmen and women are on the Highland Cattle Council in 1997. If we can get a Hill Cattle policy which favours summer grazing of cattle on our Highland hills I think the breed has a great future. Sadly, at the moment the headage payment on hill ewes has led to overstocking and overgrazing on all too many hill farms and estates. How I would love to see something that would redress this situation, but there are many more pressing problems for Government departments to attend to. I have always wanted subsidies to be used for keeping people in our hill areas, but just making the subsidies purely on the basis of headage will not help the folk who work in the hills as much as it should. The future of the breed, to my way of thinking, will be in proving to hard-headed, and all too often mean, farmers (those who wouldn't give you a blow of their handkerchief) that cross Highland cows can do the hill job really well. Not only that, they are low-input material. Although the immediate return they give in cash may not be as large as the bigger cows give, they'll cost less to keep, will live longer (a point many forget) and forage better on our windswept, wet and acid hill ground.

If Highland Beef Ltd. do as well as they predict, this will be a great step forward, as since the days (now sadly, no more) when butchers wanted bigger, older cattle, and three-year-old Highland bullocks suited that trade well, the steer side of the breed has been a headache. But let none of us fool ourselves, the B.S.E. scare will not go away, and overseas breeders I've talked to tell me that certain Governments are determined to keep our beef out. Could it have anything to do with the last war, I ask, or am I just an old cynic? But in this country too there is a growing vegetarian lobby (if only these vegetarians saw the amount of sprays those supermarket veggies get they might well consider turning instead to a succulent Highland steak from a naturally-reared steer). Because of factors like these the breed Society are in an uphill struggle to maintain their rising popularity and rising membership. If they don't succeed they will be reduced to being known only for their horns and shaggy coats as seen on post-cards, and to being seen in the flesh only outside hotels and in parks—perish the thought!

As far as the Highland folk are concerned, I know there is strong feeling against those who are termed 'White Settlers' on the part of those born and brought up in rural Highland communities. Many of these, however, have come to retire to a more tranquil way of life, and have brought their skill and tastes with them; and I have seen a tremendous change for the better in many rural districts in Scotland thanks to the 'incomers'. The obvious area of improvement is in catering and the hotel trade, where in many cases all too many hotels were really basic, and had changed little since Boswell and Johnson toured the Highlands all those two hundred plus years ago. I remember all too vividly staying in a hotel in Mull in the fifties, and seeing the water literally running down the wall in my bedroom! When I went out in the morning I saw that the gutter was full of leaves, moss and green growth: it hadn't been cleaned for years and the water was going into the room. As for the food, it reminded me of the Bible story of the prodigal son who had run away from home, spent all his money, and then wanted to return home, and it was said of him 'he would fain have filled his belly with the husks that the swine would eat'. I felt the same at this hotel, as my pigs were fed the best of skim milk, as well as the remains of the porridge that my family didn't fancy!

But forty years on, what a difference in our hotels, or at least most of them. It annoys me, though, that the Tourist Board seems to think it more important to have a telly in one's room, and other things that to my mind don't improve one's stay one bit, than to have a high standard of food provided—to my way of thinking this is what, apart from comfortable beds (with hard mattresses), the hotels should be judged on that get the accolades.

Farming, Fishing and Forestry have been the mainstays of the Highland economy for years, but nowadays tourism has taken its place along with them. Yet although the tourist season has been extended, thanks to folk of my age taking out-of-season holidays, there are months when hotels, bed-and-breakfasts, sporting activities etc. close down, whereas the three 'F's are year round occupations. Our increased scientific knowledge has brought untold improvements to all these traditional activities, but at a tremendous cost to employment opportunities. Take farming, which has been my life. When I managed hill estates after the war, one would never dream of having less than one shepherd for every five hundred ewes. He would move them out to the tops in the morning and the ewes would graze their way down the hill during the day. As you would read in one of my early chapters, the shepherd had to be physically fit to do the amount of 'gathering' required of his own and his neighbours ewes for lamb-marking, shearing, sales etc. But what happens today? A shepherd has to look after at least one thousand ewes, he usually doesn't live in a cottage situated beside his 'hirsel' of ewes (the old cottages are rented to summer visitors for vast amounts of money), he has to travel a distance to his work, but we all have cars today, and all too often the little bit of shepherding he does is on a four-wheeled Japanese motorbike. Meantime the ewes remain in one area and eat it bare, especially the young heather, and fill themselves with worms! But as far as the latter is concerned the worm doses, injections etc. we now have are marvellous compared with what we had fifty years ago. Many hill ewes are now housed at lambing time with a saving of thousands of lambs. But the sad thing is it means fewer folk are employed. I have a photo of twenty young shepherds that I gathered up at Clachan, Carndow, Argyll in the fifties, in what is now a highly successful Oyster Bar, so that they could learn to shear sheep with electric clippers instead of the hand shears that we had used for a century. I think I'm right in saying only two are still in sheep farming. I now can't see more people being employed in farming in the Highlands, in fact sadly I think there will be fewer. As I've said before and will say again and again, the headage subsidy on livestock is all wrong: the subsidy should be on labour or on the services that are essential to the survival of remote communities.

Fishing too is now highly mechanised, with millions being spent on new boats that need less man-power: they are veritable floating hotels, but they are scooping up the fish to such an extent that I wonder when all the seas will run dry of fish!

As regards forestry, there are vast areas of ghastly rectangles of sitka spruce, planted in the fifties and sixties when hill land was cheap. The Forestry Commission promised they would employ a lot of labour, but what happened? They built the cottages, which now in all too many areas have been sold off as holiday homes, and all too many of the plantations have never been properly thinned—so much for the boost to employment.

Then we come to land ownership, which has always been a hot potato in the Highlands. I have managed six Highland estates since the last war, and there is no way any of them could have been viable without financial resources from outside. In my day shipping, tobacco, whisky or banking magnates bought these estates, and now we are seeing foreign potentates coming to buy estates from countries that have nothing like our sporting potential in terms of hunting, or pheasant, partridge and grouse shooting and red deer stalking. I am in no position to say whether this is a good or a bad thing, as long as they employ as many locals as they can, but if the ever-more-powerful do-gooders succeed in letting everything that crawls, walks or flies live there won't be any more sporting estates left, and the Highlands will be immeasurably poorer in every way.

Diversification is of course the name of the game, and in Scotland the outstanding example is the Buccleuch Estate, but sadly Highland estates don't have the type of land or climate enjoyed in the Borders. However there are one ore two estates of which I have personal experience that have done a great job of diversification from the old 'sheep-only' system. Dunvegan Estates, of which I have written, have done a wonderful job of using to the full all the romanticism of the past with the practicalities of what tourists expect today. Then at Cairndow, Argyll, the Ardkinglas Estate, instead of being dependent on sheep, a few cattle and some timber sales, has blossomed into a highly successful business, with a famous oyster bar (situated in an old cow byre in which I actually hand-milked cows thirty-seven years ago!), a fish farm and a forestry unit that finishes the timber it extracts in the form of furniture etc. I know from personal experience, as I managed the Estate from 1959 to 1964, that it has certain advantages that many Highland estates do not have, but having said that, I, as Estate Factor/Manager, never saw or exploited those advantages when I was there. The staff employed now is some forty, or even more if you think of all those who supply that lovely bread you get with your oysters etc. etc. When I was there the then owners and I weren't thinking about how things were changing, as we were 'Aye Beens'.

The life-style of this country has changed dramatically since the last war, there is more money about, there is more leisure time and everyone has a car (or judging by the jams on the roads and motorways, nearly everyone). So the Highland folk have to adjust to modern attitudes and ways of thinking, as more and more want to get away from the hurly-burly of city life and visit our wonderful country with its breath-taking scenery (when it's not raining whole water!)

How I would love to finish these ramblings by saying what a marvellous future Highland ponies, cattle and folk have, but I fear their futures lie in their ability to sell themselves, and this to date has been confined to individual effort and not the concerted efforts that those who are 'bred in the Highlands' need and deserve. Take the factory at Fort William for pulping the sitka spruce which I have just written about. This was my late boss Michael Noble's idea when he was Secretary of State, but it never seemed to get off the ground as it should have done. I could cite other grandiose schemes that have attracted public money from the Highland and Islands Development Board that haven't succeeded as the proposers thought they would. The real success story has been the fish-farming industry, the way their product has been marketed and the huge number of jobs that have been created: but are the fish farms in some of our lochs which are fed by salmon rivers not spoiling the run of the natural salmon? Is the farming so successful that salmon will once again be as plentiful as it was in the last century, when the workers on the Rothiemurchas Estate on the Spey refused to work because they were being fed salmon every day, and insisted that twice a week would be more than enough?

We will see more and more individuals working from the Highlands with their computers, faxes, telephones etc., but sadly because they will come from different backgrounds they won't keep the village halls ringing as the old workers used to do, with the laughter and with the 'hoochs!' that accompanied the dancing of 'The Duke of Perth', the eightsome reels etc. at the weekly dances. Nor will they use the village shops, and they are already few and far between, because of the takeover of the supermarkets with their brilliant marketing but ghastly, impersonal queues and check-outs.

All the foregoing sounds dismal in the extreme, and are the ramblings of an 'Aye Been' who loved the old way of life he has enjoyed living and working in the Highlands for half a century. But he realises all too well that progress, so-called, is inevitable, and that the way of life in the Highlands and the people who live there will change. But thank God, literally, that our scenery, which is second to nothing I have seen in all the many overseas countries I have visited, will remain.

Also, there remains a certain liquid 'ambrosia', which only the Highlands can produce, called whisky. Through thick and thin it has been a great, if not the greatest, ambassador that the Highlands have had. And it has greatly helped me in the writing of these chapters!